D0091551

# COME TO PAPA

*Encountering The Father That Jesus Knew*

## By Gary Wiens

Unless otherwise indicated, all Scripture quotations in this publication are from *The Holy Bible,* The New King James Version. Copyright © 1979, 1980, 1982, Thomas Nelson Inc., publishers.

**Copyright © 2003 by Gary Wiens**
All rights reserved. No part of this publication may be reproduced, stored in a retrieval system, or transmitted, in any form or by any means, electronic, mechanical, photocopying, recording, or otherwise, without prior permission, except for brief quotations embodied in critical reviews and certain other noncommercial uses permitted by copyright law. For permission requests, please contact *www.burningheartministries.com.*

Printed in the United States of America on acid-free paper.
ISBN 0-9704791-5-8

**Ordering Information**
Burning Heart Ministries, Inc.
13309 Corrington Avenue
Grandview, MO 64030 USA

*www.burningheartministries.com*

816-965-9336

## DEDICATION

To my wife Mary, and our children, Dave, Alyson, and Rachel.
They were the vehicles of the Father's instruction in my life,
and have thankfully emerged from the process
loving Him and loving me.

# TABLE OF CONTENTS

# PROLOGUE:
## NEW EYES TO SEE THE FATHER

Have you ever had the experience of coming to know a familiar thing in a new way, in which the depth and scope of your understanding has shifted dramatically, and yet the foundational truth has remained the same? This is the experience that I had in the course of coming to the understandings of God as our Father that are expressed in this book. As the Holy Spirit began to stir my heart concerning these things a number of years ago, the best word picture I could generate was as though a black-and-white, two-dimensional picture had suddenly become color and three-dimensional.

In contrast to what so many have endured with regard to their relationships with fathers and father-figures, my own experience was relatively good. My father was a pastor in a small, conservative denomination, and I was raised in a reasonably healthy family environment. I met the Lord when I was ten years of age and was fingered by the Holy Spirit at seventeen for a life of preaching and church ministry. But at the same time, my experience left much to be desired, for my father was the product of a very rigid German Mennonite family, raised in a poverty-stricken rural setting during the First World War. His father was a strict and harsh man, and though he was a committed Christian, there was very little warmth in the home.

By comparison to his context, my father was much warmer

1

and more open than his father had been, but there was still a significant residue of rigidity and distance that had profound effect
on me. Like so many others, I grew up with a fear of displeasing
my dad, and earning his approval became my subconscious goal
in life. I never heard the words "I love you" from him, and though
we had time together playing baseball and golf, I had to learn from
other people in later years that he was proud of me. We became
much closer in the last years of his life, and I know that there were
many regrets on his part for how he raised his family. Much of
what I am sharing with you in this book came to me as I was in
the process of recognizing the damaging patterns in our relationship, forgiving him for his inadequacies and repenting for mine.

During my college years, I met Mary, who would become my
wife. She was raised in the same denominational atmosphere, and
though her father was a much gentler man than mine was, there
were still issues of emotional distance common to most families of
that generation and culture. Though the atmosphere of her home
was quiet and compassionate, affection was not expressed overtly,
and negative emotion was hidden and not verbalized. So, as we
began to plan for our own family, we had many discussions about
the kind of relationship we wanted to have together, and the kind
of parents we wanted to be. Most of those discussions involved
strategies about how to communicate with our children differently
than than had been modeled for us and how we would go about
affecting those changes through forgiveness and repentance. It was
in the middle of those processes, which were easy to talk about
and have taken a lifetime to implement, that the Lord began to stir
my heart with longing for the knowledge of the Father's heart. I
needed a revelation of the heart of God as Father, and in His infinite kindness, He gave me what I needed.

It is what the Apostle Paul must have had in mind when he
prayed over the Ephesian believers. He prayed that the eyes of their
hearts would be enlightened by a Spirit of wisdom and revelation,
that they might come to know in new ways the full dimensions of
God's love for them.[1] Paul's desire was that these precious saints

---

[1] See *Ephesians 1:17-19*

would be overwhelmed by the majesty of the love of God, and that their hearts would be ignited by this passionate experience.

In the Greek language, several words express our concept of "knowledge." One of these words is "*gnosis*," and it carries the meaning of an intellectual knowledge, a theoretical understanding that is not backed up with experience. This is the kind of two-dimensional, black-and-white knowledge that, even though it may be true, is nevertheless insufficient to satisfy the longings of our hearts to know the Lord.

"*Gnosis*" is the kind of knowledge that comes by explaining something to someone who has never experienced it. For example, have you ever tried explaining something like a roller-coaster ride to someone who has never been on one? Better yet, try to imagine the terrifying thrill of bungie jumping off a high bridge or white-water rafting on the Colorado River when the water is wild and high if those events have never been part of your experience.

There is another, much richer word for knowledge that is "*epignosis*." This word carries an experiential dimension to it, the sort of knowledge that comes from riding the roller coaster, taking the jump, or clinging to the raft as the freezing water knocks you silly. It is the kind of intimate knowledge that is the reality in a healthy marriage relationship, where the deep internal realities of the human soul are opened up in full trust before the partner in the context of holy romance. This is the kind of knowledge that God intends for us to have concerning Himself and His Beloved Son Jesus, and it is the release of this kind of knowledge that is the purpose of this book.

I live in Kansas City, Missouri, and have the privilege to be part of a vibrant and emerging ministry called the Friends of the Bridegroom Missions Base, under the leadership of Mike Bickle. This organization, with the International House of Prayer at its core, has as its main focus what we call the "Forerunner Ministry." All through history, God has raised up "forerunners" to prepare the way of the Lord before the release of new dimensions of His Kingdom and power. While Jesus is the only person actually

declared to be the Forerunner,[2] the clearest presentation of this in
Scripture was the coming of John the Baptist. The angel Gabriel
prophesied to John's father Zacharias that John would be the fulfillment of Malachi's prophecy, one who would turn many of the
children of Israel to the Lord their God. He will also go before Him
in the spirit and power of Elijah, 'to turn the hearts of the fathers to
the children, and the disobedient to the wisdom of the just, to
make ready a people prepared for the Lord.' (Luke 1:16)

Malachi had prophesied that there would come a release of the
Spirit that was on Elijah, an anointing to heal the curse on the land
that results from a false perception of the nature of God as our
Father. John was the embodiment of that ministry and was sent to
bring a ministry of repentance for the purpose of preparing the
way for the Messiah, Jesus. In turn, Jesus would restore a true
understanding of the Father's nature and character.

As the people would repent, turning away from the false
images of the nature and character of God, they would turn
toward the truth that was being declared day after day through the
life and ministry of Jesus. He came to reveal the Father as He really
is, to relate to all manner of people in the gentleness and faithfulness of the Father's true nature. This was so that men's hearts and
minds might again perceive Him in an accurate way. Only by this
strategy could the people begin to understand their true identity as
the sons and daughters of the Father. Only in this way would they
know that they were beloved children being prepared for a marvelous destiny – to be the Bride of the One Beloved Son, Jesus
Christ. As people began to perceive God in right ways, they would
find the courage and strength to believe that they were indeed the
Bride being prepared for the worthy Son, to be presented to Him
in the day of His power and victory.

But our destiny is not completed just by being sons and daughters of the Father. God had more in mind than simply having a lot
of little human munchkins running around heaven. His purpose
becomes clearer in Ephesians 3, verses 14-21, where Paul calls

---

[2] See *Hebrews 6:20*

upon the Father to release His Spirit. He desires that the Spirit of the Father would invade the hearts of the believers and establish them in the foundational reality of the Father's love. This is so that, being rooted and grounded in the love of the Father, we might be empowered to grow into the fullness of relationship with the Bridegroom – that we might "know the love of Christ which passes knowledge, and to be filled with all the fullness of God."

It is so essential to see that the experiential love of the Father is to be foundational to us, the root-system of our lives, and not the target of our activity. Part of the curse of fatherlessness is that the experience of the love of the Father is seen to be a target, the end-result of a faithful and fervent life. When this false perception is in place, human attempts at obedience to God are robbed of the very power that makes obedience possible. This power comes through the knowledge of His affection and love in our immaturity and weakness. When this experience of His affection is missing, we lack the very power necessary to become what we are created to be, and serving the Lord with gladness degenerates into embittered and powerless slavery.

Paul, however, makes it clear that the experience of God's love is the root-system, the foundation stone of empowered living. It releases in us the power to grow into the full experience of what He has always intended. God desires us to be joined in a relationship of intimacy with His Son that would lead to the full release of God's nature and power being infused into the human race.

The third dimension of this extravagant plan is revealed in Ephesians 5, where Paul's instructions on holy marriage find their reference point in the romantic intentions of Christ for His Bride, the Church. Husbands are told to love their wives as Christ loves the Church, and that the end result of the process is the presentation to Himself of a glorious Bride, devoid of spot or wrinkle.

This was the message that was being released through the ministry of John the Baptist. He was plowing fallow ground, the dry soil of hearts that had become hardened in the drought of a religious system devoid of romance and affection. Empowered by his own experience of the enflaming love of Jesus, John's voice was causing the high places of pride to be brought low and the low places of depression to be lifted up. His message was focused on repairing the highway of right thinking about God, so that the Son of God could walk upon that road with ease. His was the voice crying in the wilderness, demanding that a way be prepared for the coming of the Lord.

In the same way, God is raising up voices at this time in history. He is calling men and women at the end of the age that are created and anointed to declare the true nature of God as the loving Father, one who desires to draw all people to His presence. This is so that He might pour out love, healing, restoration, and justice, and prepare His people for the physical return of Jesus. This in turn is so that human history might be brought to its culmination – the marriage supper of the Lamb.

As a result of God's design established from the foundations of the earth, there have been two emphases in the heart of God released to the Body of Christ over the past 30 years or so. These messages are the two dimensions of the Forerunner message – the knowledge of the Father's heart and the declaration of the Bridal Paradigm of relationship with Jesus. This was the focus of John the Baptist – through the declaration of the reality of the Father's heart to prepare the way for the coming of the Bridegroom.

In my current role as one of the senior leaders at the Friends of the Bridegroom Missions Base in Kansas City, I spend most of my time traveling, teaching, and declaring the passionate heart of Jesus the Bridegroom for His Beloved Bride, the Church. The declaration of this message is one of the central joys of my life, and the privilege of partnering with the Holy Spirit to open the spiritual eyes of God's people is a precious and rare thing. But this current joyous thing is rooted in a knowledge of the Father's love that began to emerge in the early 1980s as the Lord began to direct my family and me into new dimensions of His love and power.

During the fall of 1985, I was pastoring a Vineyard church in Aurora, Colorado. In that season, the Holy Spirit began to release to me, in a simply sovereign and delightful way, a series of messages on the nature of the Father that were revolutionary to my experience and understanding. At that time in my life, I was coming into a friendship with a prophetic brother named Bob Jones, who then lived in Kansas City. Although Bob was and is a brilliant man, and a thorough student of the Bible, his personal style was childlike, transparent, and delightfully unsophisticated. As I spoke with him one day, I was asking him about his relationship with the Father. His response was intriguing to me. He said "Well, if I call Him Father, He just seems 'father and father away,' so I call Him 'Papa.' " So as these messages of the Father's identity and character began to form in me, I entitled the resulting teaching series "Come To Papa," with the idea of coming to know the Father that Jesus knew in the kind of intimate friendship that I saw exemplified in my friend Bob. I began to consider His character as revealed in the parables of Jesus and settled on a number of messages that eventually comprised a tape series.

In recent months, I received an exhortation from a friend that these old messages were precious, and that the foundations of the knowledge of the Father's heart still need to be laid in the hearts of millions of young men and women that the Holy Spirit will sweep into the Kingdom of God. Then, I met some old friends who had a set of the original tapes from a conference they attended in 1987, so I asked if I could borrow the tapes and listen to them again. As I did so, I was impacted by the still-fresh revelation of God's heart as the Father of His children, preparing them for an eternal relationship of delight as the Bride of His Son. I felt stirred by the Holy Spirit to re-dig these wells of revelation and to put these messages in book form so that this dimension of the Forerunner message could be established again.

My prayer is that as you read this book, the knowledge of the Father's love will capture your heart in a deep way, establishing the foundations that will release the knowledge of the love of the Bridegroom in your experience, unto being filled with all the fullness of God.

Gary Wiens
Kansas City, Missouri
August 2003

CHAPTER

# THE FATHER OF GLORY

EPHESIANS 1:17-19

**1**

Over the past number of years, the prayer of the Apostle Paul over the Ephesian church has been a key point of intercession in my own life. Jesus Himself stated in His High Priestly prayer recorded in John 17 that the real meaning of eternal life is to know the Father, and Jesus Christ, whom the Father sent to reveal Him. Paul knew the essential nature of this revelation, and so he prayed that God would release to the Ephesians "the Spirit of wisdom and revelation unto the knowledge of Him." As I have prayed this phrase many hundreds of times, I have become more convinced than ever that this is the most important experience of human existence. It is the essence of salvation and occurs when the Spirit of Christ comes to an individual, bringing revelation of who God is as our Heavenly Father. It is in the light of that revelation that every other experience comes into focus and finds its purpose.

In that little prayer from Ephesians 1:17, there is a name ascribed to the Father that simply captivates me. He is called "the Father of glory." As I have meditated over and over on that phrase, the meaning of it has grown deeper and yet more mysterious, richer and yet more inexplicable. I love just to say that name, to mull it over in my mind, to worship Him with that phrase, trying to find a hundred different ways to express its

9

essence. I know from my own experience that the more I muse upon His name – *Father of Glory* – the more the meaning of it will be unfolded to me, and the more I will be captured by His majesty.

That's how it works, you know. The more one muses, meditating on the nature and character of God, the larger He becomes. The more I consider Him, the more He wounds my heart with desire and longing to know Him more. His name is potent, filled with healing and saving grace, with the power to establish upon sure foundations those who believe on Him. David, the Psalmist and great King of Israel, wrote about that dynamic three millennia ago when he penned these words:

> **My heart was hot within me;**
> **While I was musing, the fire burned.**
> **Then I spoke with my tongue. . .**
> **(Psalms 39:3)**

So, in the first chapter of this book that is dedicated to the pleasure of musing upon the name and character of the Father, it seems right and good to begin with the marvelous name, the Father of Glory.

## What is Glory?

Having said that it is good to begin here, the first question concerns how one begins to speak of the glory of God. "Glory" is the term that is used in a general way to communicate the unspeakable aspects of God's beauty, majesty, and power. The Hebrew term, "*kabod*," is best translated "weightiness, or heaviness," and refers to that dynamic that happens when someone of authority or beauty enters a room. One immediately feels the "weight" of their presence, and there is an automatic sense of deference that is felt in the hearts of those who know or honor that person. Occasionally, there is one whose presence commands the attention of everyone, whether or not he is known or acknowledged in a personal way. It is the dynamic that happened in the experience of the Queen of

Sheba when she visited King Solomon. She had heard of his fame and majesty, but could not conceive of such greatness. So, she did the wise thing and came to see for herself. When the Queen saw this man, the Scripture says that "there was no more spirit in her," and the text goes on to quote her response at seeing Solomon for the first time:

> **Then she said to the king: "It was a true report which I heard in my own land about your words and your wisdom. However I did not believe their words until I came and saw with my own eyes; and indeed the half of the greatness of your wisdom was not told me. You exceed the fame of which I heard. Happy are your men and happy are these your servants, who stand continually before you and hear your wisdom! Blessed be the LORD your God, who delighted in you, setting you on His throne to be king for the LORD your God! Because your God has loved Israel, to establish them forever, therefore He made you king over them, to do justice and righteousness."**
> **(2 Chronicles 9:5-8)**

This woman, well-acquainted with the reality of majesty, was unprepared for the revelation of the greatness of Solomon. She saw his glory, the weight of his person and presence, the splendor of his wisdom, and she was undone. She could do nothing else than to lay all her riches before him, honoring him as great and wise above all others, placing herself under his authority. This is what happens to a person who comes face to face with glory. We are undone when we encounter it, for it opens our hearts to the fact that there is a greater reality than ourselves, one to which we owe everything.

If this is the response of a Queen to another human being, how much more are we undone as we find ourselves before the One who is called "the Father of glory!" Like Isaiah, who encountered the Presence of the Lord as he went to worship, we occasionally come unwittingly into an encounter with God's Presence. In those times, He increases the voltage just a little bit, and all we can do is tremble and weep because of the touch of His hand somewhere deep inside our souls. I remember a time during the spring of 2003 when such a situation occurred. I was at a conference in Rutland, Vermont, at the House of Worship there, and I was scheduled to speak in the first session of the conference. I had a clear sense of where I wanted to go with the teaching, and because I dearly love to talk about the Lord, was eager to get to it. However, during the prayer time before the meeting began, the Holy Spirit allowed our sense of His Presence to increase, just a little. My emotions began to surge to the forefront, for I love to experience the sense of His immediate nearness even more than I love to talk about it. As we worshipped and prayed, the weight of glory increased, and I simply started to come unglued. It continued into the meeting time, and when it was time for me to speak, I was so overcome that I felt I had absolutely nothing to say. In the most halting tones, I simply shared what was going on with me in the face of His glory, His beauty, and goodness being present with us.

These kinds of experiences are addictive to me. I love – no, I crave the Presence of the Lord, for it is in His Presence, in the immediacy of His touch upon my heart, that I know who I am. In the experience of His pleasure over me, I realize, like the Queen of Sheba, that there is One to whom is due everything I am and all that I have.

## Show Me Your Glory

Because of the joy and pleasure that is found in those kinds of experiences of God's Presence, we find ourselves drawn again and again to the place of seeking to know Him better. As I said, the Presence of the Lord is addictive, and we were designed to be captured by this addiction. We were never created to live bored, dissipated lives or to be satisfied with the inferior pleasures of temporary things. We were created to live an exhilarated existence, intoxicated with the beauty and goodness of God. We were meant to be captured by His heart, in love with the One who is madly in love with us. Because I have come to believe this with all my heart, I am an unrepentant pleasure-seeker. The place where that longing for delight is most completely satisfied is in the Presence of the Lord.

I am impacted by the yearning of Moses' heart as revealed to us in Exodus 33 and 34. This humble man dared to ask the God of power and majesty to reveal Himself to him. Indeed, Moses was adamant and refused to take "no" for an answer. He was filled with the craving to know God, to understand His ways, and to see His glory. This insatiable desire was pleasing to God, whose heart is that of an ardent romantic. Like any true lover, God desires to be desired, and those who seek after Him with longing hearts are indeed satisfied. Moses' cry was "Show me Your glory. God of heaven and earth, what is it that makes Your Presence so over-whelming? What is the essence of Your beauty, that of which the heavens sing night and day? They send their message throughout the earth in undeniable fashion, so that anyone with a heart of desire may seek You and find You.[1] Show me who You are, because the little hints You have given me up to now have merely driven me mad with desire, aching to know You more."

God was pleased with this cry from the heart of this servant who was becoming His friend. He prepared Moses in a certain way – for to gaze upon God is to die; one way or another, every-thing changes – and God caused His character to be revealed to Moses in a stunning, overwhelming manner. Consider Moses' own words in describing this encounter:

> **Now the LORD descended in the cloud and stood with him there, and proclaimed the name of the LORD. And the LORD passed before him and proclaimed, "The LORD, the LORD God, merciful and gracious, longsuffering, and abounding in goodness and truth, keeping mercy for thou-sands, forgiving iniquity and transgression and sin, by no means clearing the guilty, visiting the iniquity of the fathers upon the children and the children's children to the third and the fourth generation." (Exodus 34:5-7)**

---

[1] See *Psalm 19:1-5*

Moses sought the revelation of God's glory, that which makes Him beautiful and appealing. The Lord's response to this quest was to declare His name, "Yahweh," and to speak of His character as overwhelmingly good, kind, and merciful. There is such irresistible kindness in these words, a goodness that invites us, compels us to draw near and come to know Him better. Yahweh, the God who is what He is, simply cannot lie about anything, especially Himself. This God says that He is gracious and merciful to people in such a way that He devastates my resistance and draws from my heart the same response Moses had:

> **So Moses made haste and bowed his head toward the earth, and worshiped. Then he said, "If now I have found grace in Your sight, O Lord, let my Lord, I pray, go among us, even though we are a stiff-necked people; and pardon our iniquity and our sin, and take us as Your inheritance." (Exodus 34:8-9)**

This is the part that staggers me as I read it! Moses' conclusion to this experience of the glory of God was that somehow he knew it was his destiny, and the destiny of the people he was leading, *to be God's own inheritance!* Paul's prayer from Ephesians 1, with which I opened this chapter, has as its focus that we would come to know this unimaginable reality: God has an inheritance in the saints. Think of it! This God, this matchless Father of glory and kindness, has an inheritance, and that inheritance is *people!* Human beings with warts and all are the beings that capture the heart of God, even as our hearts are snared by Him. God's desire as the Father of all things is that we would be His inheritance, the thing that completes and satisfies His heart.

It is virtually inconceivable to me that the uncreated God could have a desire for people at all, let alone weak ones![2]  It

---

[2] I have written more completely about this in Chapter One of my book *Songs of a Burning Heart*, Tributary Music, Toronto, 2001.

becomes even more incredible when we begin to realize that His desire is to present us weak ones to His precious Son, Jesus. We are to be the gift of a counterpart, a Bride that will be the perfect helper, suitable to the perfect Son.[3] The Father of glory exercises the kindness and mercy of His very being upon us for the purpose of cleansing and preparing us to be His own inheritance. We are becoming the eternal and glorious Bride of Christ, the fullness of Him who fills everything in everything.[4]

**The Glory of God in the Face of Jesus Christ**

Precisely because of this great love and desire in His own heart, the Father of our Lord Jesus, the Father of glory, sent His Son into the world to redeem us.[5] In the process of that reclamation, Jesus reveals to us exactly what His Father is like. The writer of the letter to the Hebrew believers says it like this:

> **God, who at various times and in various ways spoke in time past to the fathers by the prophets, has in these last days spoken to us by His Son, whom He has appointed heir of all things, through whom also He made the worlds; who being the brightness of His glory and the express image of His person, and upholding all things by the word of His power, when He had by Himself purged our sins, sat down at the right hand of the Majesty on high. (Hebrews 1:1-3)**

Jesus is the Heir of all things in the Father's Kingdom, and the pinnacle of that inheritance is you and me. When He came into the world, He came to reveal the Father's character, His name, His ways. He did this so that people would recognize what kind of God we have and have our hearts captured by His desiring love. This Father of glory is a romantic, an ecstatic

---

[3] See Ephesians 5:25-32
[4] See Ephesians 1:23
[5] See John 3:16

lover[6] who is unwilling to settle for anything less than that the desire of His Son be satisfied by eternal relationship with human beings. Therefore, His strategy in sending Jesus was to reveal Himself in such a way that the hearts of human beings would be won by His love, His revealed glory. Jesus would be the revealer of the Father of glory.

There is a powerful passage in Paul's second letter to the believers in Corinth that speaks to this issue. Consider this:

**For it is the God who commanded light to shine out of darkness, who has shone in our hearts to give the light of the knowledge of the glory of God in the face of Jesus Christ. (2 Corinthians 4:6)**

Paul is saying that the same God who created the heavens and the earth, commanding the sun into existence when nothing but darkness was over the universe, has now released a light into the darkness of the human heart. The purpose of this revealing light is so that we might see the glory of God the Father in the face of His Son, Jesus Christ. In other words, the whole point of Jesus' coming to the earth the first time was to show us what kind of Father we have, the Father Jesus knows. He is not the father of empty religious systems, nor is He the kind of father who is distant or harsh. Rather, He is the Father of glory, the Father of beauty and kindness and mercy that we all long to know. His is the heart we yearn to touch, and in His embrace, we will find all that we need. Our childlike hearts echo the cry of Phillip as recorded in the eighth verse of John 14 – *"show us the Father, and that will be enough for us."*

Jesus' response to this plaintive cry was pointed and clear:

---

[6] The word *ecstasy* literally means to be "out of balance or beside one-self," usually as a result of strong, joyful emotion. In the incarnation, God literally came outside of Himself because of love, coming to earth to capture our hearts.

**Jesus said to him, "Have I been with you so long, and yet you have not known Me, Philip? He who has seen Me has seen the Father; so how can you say, 'Show us the Father'? Do you not believe that I am in the Father, and the Father in Me? The words that I speak to you I do not speak on My own authority; but the Father who dwells in Me does the works. Believe Me that I am in the Father and the Father in Me, or else believe Me for the sake of the works themselves. (John 14:9-11)**

The impact of this passage is deep and eternal. The person of Jesus is the precise definition and revelation of who the Father is. Jesus shows us what the Father is like and how He relates to weak and broken human beings. He came to reveal the Father, to make His name known, and to break down the misunderstandings and faulty images of God that had arisen over the centuries. Jesus came as the fullness of God in human form,[7] and all of His interactions with human beings perfectly demonstrated the character and nature of the Father. Jesus is the goodness of God personified, and those whose hearts were open to see this reality saw the glory of the Father revealed in the face of Jesus as He encountered people day after day.

Oh, I love to meditate on this reality! The glory of God in the face of Jesus Christ! That the God who created the heavens and the earth would cause a light to shine in my cold, dark, and chaotic heart so that I might recognize Him in the face of this beautiful Man! I am perpetually undone.

How this brings the Scriptures to life as I read the encounters between Jesus and the people He met! Each one of those encounters was specifically orchestrated by the Father for the purpose of revealing His own glory to weak human beings. I love to imagine the encounters of the Gospels, entering into the stories as a participant. I love to take the place of the main character in the story – the man at the pool in John 5 or the woman at the well in John 4. I try to imagine what they felt in their cir-

---

[7] See *Colossians 2:9*

cumstances and what happened on their insides as Jesus came
to encounter them with the glory of the Father. As I consider
His merciful and kind interactions with people such as
Zacchaeus the tax collector or the gentle but pointed exchanges
with Peter and the other disciples, I begin to realize that Jesus
will deal with me in the same merciful and gentle way. When
He comes to the leprous beggar in Mark 1, I see how the Father
feels toward the unclean places in my life. I see how willing He
is to heal me of the issues that separate me from Him and from
the rest of His people. As Jesus ministers with mercy to the
woman taken in adultery in John 8, I begin to have hope that
the places of shame in my life will be dealt with mercifully and
not with condemnation. By the same token, when I see Jesus
confronting and rebuking the Pharisees and the legalistic leaders of the religious systems of the day, I understand how He
feels about my attitudes of superiority. I begin to know how He
feels about the elitism in my heart that keeps me from being
compassionate with the broken people of the earth. The hope
that fills my heart upon consideration of these things is overwhelming to me. If God is like this man Jesus, then I want to
know Him more!

### Restoring the Knowledge of the Father

It is for this purpose that this book is being written. When the
angel Gabriel met with Zacharias the priest in the House of the
Lord,[8] he prophesied to the old man that a son would be born to
him and his wife Elizabeth. This son would be called John, and

> **"He will also go before Him in the spirit and power of
> Elijah, 'to turn the hearts of the fathers to the children,' and
> the disobedient to the wisdom of the just, to make ready a
> people prepared for the Lord." (Luke 1:17)**

[8] See *Luke 1:5-17*

John the Baptist would be the first Forerunner, the one crying out in the wilderness, calling to the people of God to prepare the way for the coming of the Lord. This preparation had to do with a call to repentance, not primarily for doing bad things, but rather to turn away from the false understanding of God that had been put forth by the religious establishment of the day. Because of the cold and dark hearts of the religious leaders, God the Father had been presented as distant, angry, and uncompassionate. By their example, God was perceived to be tight, controlling, and filled with anger instead of as the good and kind God that He really is. So John came with the assignment to hear the voice of the Bridegroom in the wilderness[9] and to be ignited with passion by the words of his Beloved. From that experiential platform, he would call the nation to repent, to turn away from wrong beliefs about God, and turn toward this One who was coming to reveal the Father's glory.

In the same way, the Holy Spirit is raising up voices at this time in history to come once again in the Spirit and power of Elijah, to restore the hearts of the children to the knowledge of the Father as He really is. God the Father is nothing like the picture presented by tightly controlled religious systems. These often proclaim a god who is mostly mad or sad and probably never glad, especially as it concerns you and me. He is nothing like the partisan god of nationalistic politics, invoked for the purpose of validating an agenda or preserving a way of life that has little or nothing to do with the character and purposes of the God of our Lord Jesus Christ. This God is the Father of glory, the Lord of heaven and earth, whose heart burns with one passionate longing. He desires that the people of every tongue and tribe and nation be redeemed by His great mercy expressed in the sacrifice of His Son, in order that the longing heart of Jesus might be satisfied at the end of the day. This is the Father that Jesus knew and the One He came to reveal.

---

[9] See *John 3:29*

## My Glory, the One Who Lifts My Head

This Father of glory, whose beauty and majesty is the focus of all true desire, has as His focus the weak and broken people of the earth. This reality is simply overwhelming, and it is absolutely true. He loves to release the knowledge of His character among those with broken hearts and contrite spirits.[10] He loves to draw them to Himself with great tenderness so they might know Him as He really is. The Father loves to impart His beauty to those who come to Him in weakness, acknowledging how much they need His mercy and grace.

There is a particular verse of Scripture that touches my heart in a tender way. Recorded in Psalm 3:3, this verse beautifully ties together the experience of the glory of the Lord with the lifting of the head of one who is troubled and despairing. Consider these words:

**But You, O LORD, are a shield for me,**
**My glory and the one who lifts up my head.**

The picture that comes to my mind as I muse upon this verse causes me to remember the dilemma that Eve experienced in the Garden of Eden after she had sinned. Had she obeyed the command of God, it would have resulted in her glorification by His grace. As part of the curse spoken to her as judgment for her sin, the Lord said these words:

**Your desire shall be toward your husband,**
**and he shall rule over you. (Genesis 3:16)**

What is pictured in this verse is the reality that in the sin of Adam and Eve, something very precious and important was lost. Until that point, the two had stood face to face with God, talking with Him, walking with Him in the cool of the day. They were

---

[10] See *Psalm 34:18*

His partners in managing the new creation. In due time, He would have spoken to them of all things and would have bestowed upon them the fullness of His glory. He had created them for His own desire, as the Bride of His Son. Therefore, He had the full intention of bringing them to a place of identity and fulfillment that they simply could not imagine, even in their pre-fallen condition. God would have revealed Himself to them in increasing fashion as He trained and prepared them to take the place for which they were made – joint heirs with the Son, full partners in the Kingdom of God.

But in their rebellion, a tragic thing occurred. Having stood straight up in the Presence of the Lord, they now became bent toward one another, looking to one another for the things they could only get from God. In the curse upon the woman, God said, "your desire shall be toward your husband." In other words, you are going to look to him for fulfillment, and there will be a perpetual frustration of that desire because you were never intended to gain fulfillment from merely human relationships. We were built for God, and He is the only One who meets the requirements of the heart. But because of sin, we have become bent and now look for identity and destiny in places where those things cannot be found.

In our brokenness, in our fallen state, we fix our eyes horizontally, searching for some way to gain meaning for our lives. We look to human relationships, to the workplace, the sporting arena, the human leaders who are over us in order to try to fill the longing in our hearts for significance and destiny. We are particularly bent toward our own parents, and especially our fathers, who in their brokenness cannot fulfill that for which our hearts crave. Hear this now – they not only do not fill that place, they cannot. We were never intended to be made full in mere horizontal relationships. The yearning that exists inside the human heart has a God-shape to it, and only the Father of glory can release to us the reality that gives our lives their fullness.

We humans instinctively know that we are meant to be glorious. It is the residue of the divine image that, while broken, is nevertheless still there inside us. We know we ought to matter, that someone ought to love us unconditionally. We know instinctively that we are incapable of defining ourselves in a satisfactory way, and so we constantly look to things or people outside ourselves to fill that place of desire. Because of sin, we are bent toward one another, desiring from one another that which cannot be obtained there.

What the Father of glory desires to say to us is this: "I am your glory; I am the One who defines you, and the One who imparts to you all your significance. If you will come to Me, I will lift your head again, I will raise your eyes from that bent position. I will cause you to gaze upon Me, the One able to save you and restore you into being the person I created you to be."

It is the Heavenly Father who knows who we are, and who alone has the power to speak that identity into our hearts. His definition of us is the only one that is real and the only one that really matters. Every definition that we try to put upon our lives is inadequate. Every definition that is placed upon us by other people or other entities in horizontal relationship is untrue, except to the extent that it agrees with the Father's opinion. He alone defines me, and He alone has the power to impart the glory that I instinctively know is mine.

God is very smart. We are told in Proverbs 25:2 that *"it is the glory of God to conceal a matter, and the glory of Kings to search out a matter."* The meaning of that verse in this context is that God has given to each one of us a small portion of understanding concerning who we are and the place that we have in His heart. That small portion is just enough for us to be aware that we ought to be great. Though it may be obscured by pain or circumstance, every person has that internal sense that we were designed to reign as kings and queens, joint heirs with the Son of God. In other words, we have just enough information to make us hungry for more.

Because God's primary desire is intimate relationship with us, He has hidden the major portion of this understanding in His own heart. This information is not kept hidden out of contempt, in order to frustrate us. Rather, it is hidden precisely because part of God's nature as the Father of glory is to conceal precious things, like hidden treasure. Then, He tells us that the major part of our identity will be discovered as we draw near to Him. Our glory as kings, as joint heirs with Jesus, is to search out these riches hidden in His heart. As we come to Him, seeking the knowledge of His name, the Father opens His heart to us and begins to speak to us of who we are to Him. He lifts our heads so that we may gaze upon His beauty and goodness, and then speaks to us of identity, value, and purpose. Through speaking to us by His Spirit, the Father establishes us in the glory that reflects His own. In this way, everyone gets what they want! God gets intimate relationship with us as His inheritance, the Bride for His Son Jesus. We get what we long for – the knowledge that we are infinitely and unconditionally loved, that our lives have meaning, that an eternal destiny of significance is our portion. What wisdom and grace belong to Him!

**The Glory of the Servant**

The more we experience this growth in intimacy with the Father, the more we become partners with Christ. We begin to share in the ministry of this message of reconciliation and hope. We become the Bride who speaks with the authority of the Father and the Son, calling to one another to draw near and enter into this romance of the ages. From the intimate place of Bridal identity, we become free to express our lives in the servant-nature of Jesus. It was Jesus, clothed in servant's garb, who most clearly portrayed the glory of the Father through His suffering, death, and resurrection.

As Jesus drew near to the end of His days on earth, He began to speak of the revelation of God's glory and the reality of His own suffering and death in the same sentences. This was profoundly disturbing to the disciples, for whom glory had always meant dominance and victory. The Messiah, the King of Glory,[11]

---

[11] See *Psalm 24:7-10*

would ride triumphantly through the city gates, and all the
nations of the earth would bow before His Presence and pay Him
honor. However, in their anticipation of that day – which will certainly come at the end of the age – they missed something essential. They couldn't comprehend the idea that the Servant of the
Lord must suffer and be killed at the hands of evil men. The disciples had no grid, no frame of reference by which to define glory
in those terms.

Jesus, however, perfectly understood that His glory was to
reveal the heart of the Father, to portray Him exactly as He is.
Therefore, as He approached the time of His betrayal and suffering, Jesus' prayer was that the glory of the Father would be
revealed:

> **"Now My soul is troubled, and what shall I say? 'Father,
> save Me from this hour'? But for this purpose I came to
> this hour. Father, glorify Your name." Then a voice came
> from heaven, saying, "I have both glorified it and will glori-
> fy it again." (John 12:27-28)**

It is essential that we see that this prayer for the glory of the
Father to be revealed through the life of Jesus was specifically
related to His own suffering and death. Jesus' primary purpose
in His first coming was to reveal the character and nature of the
Father, so that people would know what kind of God they have.
In His journey to the cross, Jesus was giving the most profound
and the clearest declaration of the nature of God as the Father of
glory. This Father is the One who takes upon Himself the sins of
the world.

This reality is forcefully presented in Philippians 2:5-11,
although the power of that passage has been obscured through
some unfortunate translations of the text. Allow me to quote my
own translation, at which I have arrived after much study and
prayer:

> **Let this mind be in you, which was also in Christ Jesus,
> Who, precisely because He was in the form of God, did not**

**regard this divine equality as something to be used for His own advantage. Instead, He emptied Himself by taking the form of a slave, appearing in the likeness of men. And being found in appearance as a man, He humbled Himself and became obedient to the point of death, even the death of the cross. On account of this, God also has highly exalted Him, and given Him the Name which is above every name, that at the Name of Jesus every knee should bow, of those in heaven, and of those on earth, and of those under the earth, and that every tongue should confess that Jesus Christ is Lord, to the glory of God the Father.**

Precisely because Jesus was just like His Father, He took the form of a servant, and came in the likeness of men. There was no breakdown of identity here, no contradiction to the character of God. Jesus insisted on the right to act exactly like the Father, and the glory of the Lord was revealed in a profound way. In the suffering and death of Jesus, the world saw in raw and extreme clarity the essential nature of the glory of God. He is the God who takes on the sins of the world, who stands in the place of brokenness and death for us, embracing every incident of sin and shame, absorbing into Himself the punishment of the guilty, and thereby becoming the author of salvation for everyone, anyone who will come and acknowledge that "God was in Christ reconciling the world to Himself."[12] In the aftermath of that humility and devastation, God exalted the Son to the highest place of Lordship that exists, and every knee will bow in acknowledgment of His wonder and worth.

This is the kind of Father we have. He is a Father of extreme beauty, goodness, and kindness, full of mercy and grace toward those who will place their trust in His name. He is the One who tells me who I am, who claims me as His own. It is the Father who prepares me for the destiny that He had in mind from the foundations of the earth. He is my glory, and the One who lifts

---

[12] See *2 Corinthians 5:17-21*

my head from being fixated on earthly things, so that I might gaze upon Him who is my delight. He is the Father of our Lord Jesus Christ, the Father of glory.

My prayer as you read this book is that the eyes of your heart will be enlightened by the Spirit of wisdom and revelation. I pray that you may know this glorious Father as Jesus knows Him. I pray that as you grow in the knowledge of Him, the transforming power of His Spirit will thrill you and exhilarate you all the days of your life.

## CHAPTER 2

# THE SEARCHING FATHER
## LUKE 15:1-7

The dramatic context for telling stories could hardly have been more excellently choreographed. The tax collectors and sinners had drawn near to Jesus in order to hear His teaching. The Pharisees and teachers of the Law were gathered as well, in order that they might find fault with Him to accuse Him.

I picture this event happening at the home of Matthew the tax collector, and it was perhaps his circle of friends and acquaintances that made up the guest list at the party. With the eyes of my imagination, I can see the courtyard around Matthew's home that could have been the setting for dinner. I see the scandalized religious leaders lurking outside the gates, peering in with distressed fascination. "This man receives *sinners* and eats with them!" was the statement they made. They were aghast at the audacity of Jesus to disregard the protocol of the day.

The term "sinners" is an interesting one here. In the vocabulary of the culture, the word "sinners" was used to describe a class of people who had become disconnected from the stringent organized religious system put forth by the Jews. "Sinners" were not necessarily involved in gross behavior. Often they were those who had simply voted "no" on religion, wearied by the demands and legalism of the system. They were out of the fold, backslidden people who desired relationship with God, but who found no hope within the confines of religious structure.

The fact that scandalized the Jewish leaders was that it was this group of people with whom Jesus loved to associate. He was at ease with them, and one of the most telling realities of the New Testament is that they were apparently comfortable in His presence. With the sensitivity to the Father's Spirit that characterized all His life and ministry, Jesus perceived the situation as one in which all who had ears to hear would receive truth deep into their hearts. So He launched into a series of parables, all of which were designed to reveal the Father's heart to both groups in attendance – the religious leaders on the one hand and the disenfranchised group on the other.

The three parables of Luke 15 are all focused on this eclectic crowd. In the parables of the lost sheep and the lost coin, Jesus is addressing the "sinners" and the religious leaders in that order. In the third parable, Jesus brings the two groups together and declares over them the essential unity that exists in the heart of the Father toward them. The religious ones and the sinners are all part of the same household, and both have become estranged from the Father. He is in fact very different than either group perceives Him — far more gracious, patient, kind, and merciful than they can imagine. He is the searching Father, the embracing Father, and He is about to reveal His true colors.

In this chapter, I want to draw your attention to the first of these three parables, commonly known as the Parable of the Lost Sheep. Who among us has not taken comfort in the imagery of Jesus carrying the lamb on His shoulders? We love to see Him as the tender shepherd who has left the ninety-nine to rescue the one that was lost. It's a picture that is lovely in its simplicity and power.

However, I want to take a different approach to this parable and that is to focus our meditation on the heart of the Father that is revealed here. Jesus' own testimony was that He was always about the Father's business. In fact, He never did anything except in response to the Father's initiative.[1] Therefore, we can draw the

---

[1] See such passages as *John 5:1-20* and *Mark 1:35-39*

conclusion that the compassion that motivated the Shepherd in this passage is rooted in the Father's heart. The Father's compassion is expressed by the willingness of the Son to "seek and to save that which was lost." This parable is, at bottom line, about the Father's heart and His unwillingness to allow a single one to perish without being profoundly pursued.

Let me remind you once again of the setting in which Jesus is telling this story. He is at a dinner party, and the main group that is gathered is that group known as "tax-collectors and sinners." These are the dregs of Jewish society. On the one hand, there are the ones who collaborated with the Romans to defraud the Jews of their money. On the other hand were those who simply were unable and unwilling to try to keep up with the religious demands of Jewish tradition. They were ritually unclean, and so for Jesus, as a Rabbi, to associate with them was profoundly disturbing to the religious leaders. I can imagine them gathered in little clusters around the perimeter of the meeting area, watching with shock and disgust.

The main reason for their discomfort was that Jesus was eating with these people. In that culture, there was no such thing as casually "doing lunch" with people who were ritually unclean. Eating together was serious business. It was a covenant thing because in the Jewish culture to eat together meant that you were sharing the same life-source. It meant that you were making a statement of relationship and commitment. It was precisely the statement that Jesus intended to make – *"I have come that they (the lost and disenfranchised) might have life, and have it more abundantly!"* (John 10:10).

Here is the part that was most distressing to the Jewish leaders: Jesus was doing these things *in the Name of the Father!* He was making clear statements that He and the Father were one entity. He insisted that His attitudes and actions were revealing the Father's heart for broken people. This claim had disastrous implications for the Pharisees and teachers of the Law. It exposed their styles of ministry as mere religious activity with no actual connection to the heart of God. Religious leaders don't like to face that sort of thing, and they were furious about it.

In this setting, Jesus is quick to discern the tension and discomfort that surrounds Him. So, He tells a story about a shepherd who leaves the flock to find one that was lost. An interesting fact about this story is that it beautifully illustrates the excellent gift of teaching that Jesus exercised as a Rabbi. In the educational circles of the day, there was a teaching style known as "the principle of *remes*." Because those who were students of the Scriptures knew the symbolism so well, a Rabbi would often simply make reference to a Scriptural principle. The students would then make all the connections in their minds and know exactly what the teacher was inferring. It was essentially the kind of thing that Peter did at Pentecost when he said, "this is that which the Prophet Joel spoke about . . . ," at which point everyone in the crowd knew exactly what he was referencing.

Here, Jesus is dialing up one of the oldest and clearest of Scriptural analogies. He is telling the story of Israel being the flock of God, who is the good Shepherd. Perhaps no Psalm is more loved than Psalm 23, that lovely and comforting passage assuring the tender care of the Shepherd of the flock. In Psalm 95, the hauntingly beautiful call to worship reminds us again how Israel is called "the people of God, the sheep of His pasture."

Furthermore, the leaders of Israel had come to be called "shepherds." They stood under the authority of the one Good Shepherd as those responsible in a secondary way for the well-being of the people. The Scriptures contain numerous passages such as Ezekiel 34 and Jeremiah 23, which refer to the shepherds of Israel. These passages call them to account for their behavior as leaders that did not reflect the character of God. Therefore, when Jesus began telling this parable using the principle of *remes*, by the time He had spoken a dozen words, everyone in the crowd knew that He was speaking to the leaders. He was now addressing the Pharisees and teachers of the Law positioned around the courtyard and speaking to them as the shepherds of the flock.

Jesus said:

**Suppose one of you has a hundred sheep, and loses one of them, does He not leave the ninety-nine in the open country and go after the lost sheep until He finds it? And when He finds it, He joyfully puts it on His shoulders and goes home and calls his friends and neighbors together and says; rejoice with me, I have found my lost sheep. I tell you that in the same way, there is more rejoicing in heaven over one sinner that repents, then over ninety-nine righteous persons who do not need to repent. (Luke 15:1-7)**

## How Sheep Get Lost

There are several elements in this parable to which I would draw your attention. The first question that comes to my mind is this: how does the sheep come to be lost? In musing over this and other passages that use the analogy of sheep as the people of God, we can come to see several reasons why the this little lamb got lost.

In the first place, it is the nature of sheep to wander away. I have never worked with sheep directly, but as a teenager growing up in Oklahoma, I did work with cattle from time to time. I tell you, cattle are dumb! They will just do what they jolly well feel like doing unless you have a big stick and some way of heading them off. I have heard that sheep are like that as well. In Isaiah 53, there is a little statement about sheep. It says, *"All we like sheep have gone astray; we have turned, every one, to his own way. . . ."* That verse gives an understanding of what sheep are like.

I've been told that sheep have no common sense whatsoever. For example, you can place some sort of barrier at the doorway to a sheepfold so that the first three or four sheep have to jump over this barrier to get into the sheepfold. Then you can remove the barrier and every sheep will jump over a barrier that is not there, simply because the one before it jumped. It's how sheep are. They follow blindly sometimes, just because someone else did something.

A sheep, left to its own devices, will graze its way right off a cliff. It points its nose down into the grass and will just walk right off a cliff in the pursuit of food. This is why sheepdogs are so important to a shepherd – simply to watch over these animals that seem to have no brains. There is an old hymn that says, "prone to wander, Lord, I feel it!" There is a tendency toward wandering in the inner being of sheep that gets them in trouble. That is why the Scripture says all of us "like sheep" have gone astray. Each of us has turned to his own way because that's what sheep do. They are kind of dumb.

Have you ever been in a situation where you just made a dumb decision? Not just a wrong decision, but also a dumb one? I have, and then in the aftermath, I would ask myself, "now why did I do that?" The answer is because in that moment I got the anointing of dumb that is natural to sheep. This particular sheep has known what it is to need the ministry of really good sheepdogs in my life. I love the imagery that Bible teacher Malcolm Smith has used in his exposition of Psalm 23:6. That passage speaks of Goodness and Mercy following me all the days of my life. Malcolm calls Goodness and Mercy the sheepdogs of the Good Shepherd. They follow us around, keeping us out of disaster simply because the Shepherd loves the sheep. I love that picture and am so grateful that the Lord watches out for this silly lamb!

Do you know anybody like that? This is one way sheep get lost – they just start wandering away from the main flock and heading off into what looks like a good direction. There seems to be green grass over there! So they just point their nose in that direction and go without any sense of what the flock is doing or any sense of where the shepherd is leading. Dumb.

There is another reason why sheep wander away. Sometimes it is because the shepherds do not reflect the heart of the true Shepherd of the flock. One can almost feel the tension around the circle as Jesus goes on with the parable. One of the very familiar biblical passages that uses the analogy of shepherds and sheep is Ezekiel 34, where God is speaking a scathing rebuke to Israel's leaders precisely because they were not reflecting the heart of

God in relationship to the people. The passage is as follows:

> And the word of the LORD came to me, saying, "Son of man, prophesy against the shepherds of Israel, prophesy and say to them, 'Thus says the Lord GOD to the shepherds: "Woe to the shepherds of Israel who feed themselves! Should not the shepherds feed the flocks? You eat the fat and clothe yourselves with the wool; you slaughter the fatlings, but you do not feed the flock. The weak you have not strengthened, nor have you healed those who were sick, nor bound up the broken, nor brought back what was driven away, nor sought what was lost; but with force and cruelty you have ruled them. So they were scattered because there was no shepherd; and they became food for all the beasts of the field when they were scattered. My sheep wandered through all the mountains, and on every high hill; yes, My flock was scattered over the whole face of the earth, and no one was seeking or searching for them." (Ezekiel 34:1-6)

In this parable in Luke 15, Jesus is probing right to the heart of God's controversy with the religious leaders of the day. They were self-focused, feeding and clothing themselves, and not feeding the flock. They were treating the flock with force and cruelty, not strengthening them or healing them. They were not bringing them back or seeking for the lost. And these accusations are not only appropriate for that century. These are indictments that stare the shepherds of God's flock in the face today. This passage brings pain to my own heart, for there was a time when I was a shepherd like that. My leadership brought deep confusion and pain to those who looked to me to feed them with the bread of heaven. I had focused on my own validation before God and used my leadership position as a means to that end. I was a bad shepherd, and the Lord called me to account in no uncertain terms. He removed me from leadership for a season and forcefully addressed the issues in my life that caused me to abuse His people. God is serious about this business of being shepherds after His own heart.

Whatever the reasons are that sheep come to be lost, the point of Jesus' story is that the true Shepherd is filled with desire to find them again and to restore them to His fold. Jesus had a startling message to the flock of Israel who had wandered away from God because of foolishness, or rebellion, or offense against the system. Jesus was saying, "My Father's heart is not like that of the shepherds you are accustomed to! My Father's heart is filled with love, and He is determined to find you and bring you to Himself!" He spoke to leaders with inviting tenderness yet with pointed clarity, "I am calling you to account for your leadership style! It is time to consider how you have handled God's beloved people, and repent from your abusive leadership that times of refreshing might come for the people."

### The Motivation of the Shepherd

The second major question that comes to me in considering this passage has to do with the motivation of the Shepherd to go and find this one foolish sheep. What moved His heart in such a way that finding and restoring one lone sheep was the cause of major rejoicing and celebration in the Shepherd's heart?

In meditating on this passage over the years, I have come to a settled conclusion. The primary factor that stirred the heart of Jesus to tell this story is the incredible reality of the romance conceived in the heart of the Father from the foundations of the earth. It has always been the Father's plan to give to His beloved Son a Bride. He plans to give Jesus a perfect counterpart that will satisfy all the chosen longings of the heart of God. The reason that God is not willing for any to perish[2] is that each individual is designed to be a perfect part of the Body of Christ, which will become His Bride at the end of the age. Satan has brought about rebellion, sin, and death, but the heart of God is filled with compassionate and jealous determination to have this people for Himself. The Father is determined to remove every barrier so that people can choose

---

[2] See *2 Peter 3:9*

relationship with Him if they will. His ultimate plan is to present this perfected people to His beloved Son on that day as a Bride perfectly prepared for a Son who is worthy! Wow!

The reason that Jesus is in this situation of Luke 15, telling this story, is because the Father has the heart of the tender Shepherd who will not be satisfied as long as there is one not in the fold. In this story, we are seeing the revelation of the Father's heart, and I want to suggest several things about Him.

First of all, He is one that goes after lost sheep. God is the one who takes initiative, the one who starts things in motion looking for His lost people. The dynamic here is that even one little sheep is not insignificant to Him, and He is quite willing to leave the flock to go find the one. You see, none of us has gone looking for God. The Scripture tells us that He came looking while we were still enemies, still dead in our sins.[3] Before there was even a flicker of life in our dead hearts, Jesus began to call our names. He sends His Spirit across time and space and speaks deeply into the hearts of His wandering sheep. He ignites a spark of longing, a flicker of desire by which we can begin to respond to His voice calling us in our lost state.

James 4 tells us God has made the human spirit that lives within us to earnestly, jealously long for Him. He has put a homing device in our hearts. He has created a space there that is set apart for Him. God has placed a little chip in our inner being that responds to His stimulus so that when He calls your name you might respond to Him. He takes initiative, and that is what causes you to seek after Him, to desire Him, to want to come to Him. It is in the heart of every little child to come to Papa, running joyfully into His arms. It is in the heart of every little lamb to be carried and held by the Father, by the Good Shepherd. It is in your heart!

Maybe you have had that desire frustrated or turned off. Maybe the longing to respond to His voice has been squelched by harsh treatment at the hands of uncaring fathers. Maybe that longing has been buried under the frenzied search for satisfaction in

[3] See *Ephesians 2:1*

lesser things. But I tell you the truth – the Heavenly Father is a good Shepherd. He takes initiative with you in a way that is rooted in desire and longing for you. This Father wants to know you and set you in the safety of His presence that you might come to know Him as He really is. In that place you will then come to know yourself as you truly are and that truth will set you free.

Perhaps you have had the experience of losing a child for a moment. Perhaps you even have known the horror of the death of a child. I cannot imagine any greater horror than for one of my children to become lost or to have their life stolen prematurely. I was recently talking with a good friend of mine, a member of the home group that my family is part of in Kansas City. This friend had been with his family at Daytona Beach, Florida, for a vacation and at one point realized they didn't know where their nine-year-old daughter was. Their hearts were gripped with the terror of considered possibilities, and they spent more than an hour searching for her among the tens of thousands of people that packed the beach that day. Thankfully, as the beach patrol spread the word about a lost little girl, a kind woman found Olivia crying in her terrified isolation and brought her back to the appointed spot. The relief and joy that filled the hearts of her parents was in direct proportion to the panic they had felt only moments earlier. The Father's heart is filled with desire and longing for His lost sheep, who are really His lost children. We are the future Bride of His precious Son, and He will do anything to find us. He is the God who takes initiative as the searching Father.

I want you to feel the safety, joyfulness, and relaxation that is in this truth. It is the style of the Father to go after His sheep until He finds them. It is His pleasure, it is His purpose to find them, for He is a persistent, determined, seeking God. In Luke 19:10 Jesus declared that the whole purpose of His coming was to seek and save the lost. Some of you know how persistent He is because He has come and gotten you from a far distance. In Matthew 15:24 when Jesus was dialoging with the woman about healing her daughter, He said, "Look, I came for the lost sheep of Israel, that is why I am here." His whole purpose was to find the lost sheep of

Israel. He never gives up, and He will find His sheep.

There is a second and even more profound reason why the Father will stop at nothing to find the lost sheep. The Father's heart is determined to rescue His lost sheep because His own beloved Son became the Lamb. He is the one who took on the identity of the lost ones and became lost that He might know what it is like to be away from the Father. I want you to hear this. Open up your hearts now and hear this next section. The Father is determined to find His sheep because He knows what it is to be lost. Consider this passage in Isaiah 53:

**Who has believed our report?**
**And to whom has the arm of the LORD been revealed?**
**For He shall grow up before Him as a tender plant,**
**And as a root out of dry ground.**
**He has no form or comeliness;**
**And when we see Him,**
**There is no beauty that we should desire Him.**
**He is despised and rejected by men,**
**A Man of sorrows and acquainted with grief.**
**And we hid, as it were, our faces from Him;**
**He was despised, and we did not esteem Him.**
**Surely He has borne our griefs**
**And carried our sorrows;**
**Yet we esteemed Him stricken,**
**Smitten by God, and afflicted.**
**But He was wounded for our transgressions,**
**He was bruised for our iniquities;**
**The chastisement for our peace was upon Him,**
**And by His stripes we are healed.**
**All we like sheep have gone astray;**
**We have turned, every one, to his own way;**
**And the LORD has laid on Him the iniquity of us all.**
**He was oppressed and He was afflicted,**
**Yet He opened not His mouth;**
**He was led as a lamb to the slaughter,**
**And as a sheep before its shearers is silent,**
**So He opened not His mouth.**
**(v. 1-7)**

Revelation 13:8 tells us that the Lamb of God was slain from the foundations of the earth. The plan of God from all eternity was to place every sin, all brokenness, every instance of guilt and shame on His own Son. He did this for both the victims and the perpetrators. He took all the anguish of the world upon Himself and became separate from the Father. The meaning of the incarnation of Jesus, His coming to earth in the flesh, was precisely so that He could die in our place. He is the Lamb of God offered up as the burnt offering, the holocaust that purchased our lives. In the Garden of Gethsemane, when Jesus entered into intercession, when He stepped into our place as the guilty one, He became lost for us, and the enemy had full access to Him. As He hung on the cross, found guilty of the sins of the world, the Father turned His back on Him. God allowed His own Son to receive in His body the penalty of His full wrath concerning sin. Jesus became the lost and condemned sheep, fully assuming all guilt and punishment for every human being for all time.

It is for this reason that we can find hope even in our places of brokenness. Jesus, in taking all our sorrows, all our shame and despair, in fact experienced every situation that causes us pain. God the Father, for the sake of loving you and me, allowed His own Son to experience the horror of all we have done and all that has been done to us. God visited upon Jesus the penalty of our sin and made Him to be the lost Lamb.

As I have meditated on this reality over the past years, the Father has continued to unlock my own heart to touch the fringes of His agony in allowing Jesus to take this place. The following poem is a fruit of that meditation, an attempt to touch the Father's heart.

### WHAT NIGHT IS LIKE THIS NIGHT?

**What night is like this night
when my own heart is wrenched in deepest pain?
My Son, my joy is calling for my aid,**

and I am held at bay by ageless plan
unfolding there in garden dim,
where He is cast upon the stone.
From age to age my full delight
has been poured out on this eternal Youth,
His form my very Word,
His glory my own Light.
I danced to bring Him forth,
from evermore my constant Song
Who thrilled with me at wondrous plan to win a Bride,
undeterred by purchase price – His blood, His life.

What death is like this death
as Light of life, by darkness' pow'r not once obscured,
submits His radiance to Death's designs
and makes the wickeds' grave His own;
as perfect love, not once disturbed, is interrupted there
by weight of stagg'ring pain,
and counts it joy.

And I am bound by my own joy to leave Him there,
His terror mounting as He prays;
His sweat and blood flow mingling down
as struggling to die He grips the cup.
So I will count Him guilty now,
and turn my face that Death might have his way,
betraying kiss His next reward.

What night is like this night?[4]

In one of the most profound prophetic pictures of the Old Testament, the Father gave us an insight into the passion of His own heart. It's a story that is scarcely comprehensible unless it is approached from the perspective of God's own tender heart as the Father of the one who became the sacrificial Lamb.

Found in Genesis 22, this story records a time when God

---

[4] © Gary Wiens, December, 2001

came to Abraham, to whom He given the promise of becoming the father of many, the father of nations. God's word to Abraham had been clear: these descendants would come from the blessed union between Abraham and Sarah. This would truly be a miraculous situation indeed, since both people were old, well beyond the age of child-bearing. The story is familiar, but there is a place of understanding that has come to me only recently.

I have always puzzled over the sudden and almost unintelligible command from God to Abraham. God is demanding that he take his son, his only son, Isaac, whom he loved, and present him to the Lord as a burnt offering. I can hardly imagine the emotions that must have surged through Abraham's soul! His experience with God was profound, and God had shown Himself to be not like all the other gods of the time. He was a God of mercy and compassion, tender in His dealings with people, and determined to show favor to this faithful old man.

But now, this God was demanding the unthinkable! Slay your precious son, and give him to Me as a sacrifice! I can only touch the very edges of what Abraham must have felt as he wrestled through this command. His process must have been extraordinary because at the end of his struggle, he came to the conclusion that God's plan must be to raise Isaac from the dead. Therefore, Abraham would trust this God and obey Him to the uttermost. I am awestruck at his ability to answer Isaac's question on the way to Mount Moriah. When the young man inquired about the sacrifice, Abraham's reply was this: "God will provide Himself, the Lamb."

The force of the Hebrew language there is profound. It is not "God will provide for Himself a lamb," but "God will provide Himself, the Lamb." The provision God made was to insert Himself, in the person of His Son, into the place of the sacrifice, taking the payment for sin upon Himself, thereby setting the guilty free. The Father's strategy in asking this of Abraham was to invite this father of the faith to experience what God Himself was experiencing. God Himself knew the terror and agony of giving His own precious Son as the payment in full for the sin of mankind. Abraham touched the heart of God by his willingness to trust Him. He established an eternal identity as the father of all the faithful. Our Father knows the pain of being the lost lamb because His own Son became the lost Lamb.

A number of years ago, I asked the Lord to teach me about this in a personal way and had an experience that was profound. I had received a call from a friend who was the wife of another pastor in our city. Her husband was out of town, and she had been battling with depression and overwhelming fear. She had been told, "You can't afford to be depressed now, so just pull things together and manage until your husband gets back." She could not manage. She had lost it, and when she called me on the phone, the desperation in her voice was clear.

Perhaps you know about that kind of dilemma. I am not a depressive person and do not really struggle with fear like that, but I felt as though the Lord was going to show me what to do. I arranged to meet with her and a friend who was with her. As we met together, I put my arms around her and just allowed her to come unglued. As she wept, I prayed, and she began to release the pressure that comes with having to cope when you don't have the resources to cope. That is a dreadful place, to be sure.

As I prayed over her, I sensed the Holy Spirit invite me to "share her burden." We're told in Galatians 6 to "bear one another's burdens," but I had never applied that verse in a personal ministry context such as this one. So I prayed a prayer something like this:

"Father, I ask that You would allow this sister to take on Your wholeness that is in me, and allow me to carry her pain to the cross."

Just that simple prayer. I prayed over her for a few more moments, and she said she was feeling some of the burden lifting from her spirit. I told her I would check back with her later in the day, and we went on our ways. By the time I got back to my home, I was sick. I was feverish and shaking uncontrollably. My head was throbbing with pain as I stumbled into the house, called Mary, and asked her to pray for me. I told her what had happened, and she prayed for me and just held me for awhile. I felt the heaviness lift somewhat, so I went to lie down. I knew the Lord was doing this, so I put some worship music on the tape player and began to ask the Lord to show me what was happening.

What came into my heart was something like this: He said, *"Now you know my heart, now you know what it is to hurt like they hurt and feel the agony of pain. Now you know just a touch. I want you to know that when I went to the cross I became all of that, not just for one but also for every person in the world. That is what I did, not just for you but for everyone, I took your death that you might have my life."*

The agony that caused Jesus to sweat blood was because He exchanged His life for our death. I just felt terrible. I was weeping because of the insight the Lord was giving me. I was shuddering and trembling with the burden of this thing, and so I called another friend to come over and pray for me. As he prayed and we shared together, the situation subsided, and within just a few minutes, I was back to normal.

I was in contact with that sister later that evening and over the next several days, and she was fine. Her spirit was strengthened, she was able to do what she needed to do, and the Lord just healed her. I want you to know that that is the Father's heart for you. He longs to take you in His arms and hold you and let you drink His life while He takes on your death and your sickness and your garbage. If you don't know that kind of Father, you don't know God. If that is not your Shepherd then you have not met the Good Shepherd. Not only does He see the lost sheep, not only does He understand them, not only does He go and pursue them, but when He finds them He pours the oil of the Holy Spirit on their wounds, puts them on His shoulders, carries them close and takes them home to the great celebration. Then He calls all the friends together and says, "Hey, I found the sheep! Come on over and lets have a party!" That is the Father's heart, and He longs to share it with you.

One of the songs on the tape I played that day I first prayed for that sister was by Michael Card. I don't remember the title, but the lyrics were recorded when I preached this message in the aftermath of that experience. The song goes like this:

> Never was love so tender, never was love so strong
> Even in His surrender, His love would carry on.
> And as His heart was breaking, He was mending lives;
> And as He hung there, dying, He was giving us life.
>
> So when you are tired and empty;
> when you can't run any longer
> He will take you to the finish,
> 'cause His love is stronger.
>
> Never was love so humble, never was love so great.
> The chains of death all crumbled
> as love rolled the stone away.
> And as He reigns in glory, He's still mending lives.
> And when your heart is dying, He will give you new life.
>
> So when you are tired and empty,
> when you can't run any longer
> He'll take you to the finish, 'cause His love is stronger.
>
> Take my hand as I take His; we will finish together.
> Holding on to His every word, His promise is forever.
>
> So when you are tired and empty,
> when you can't run any longer.
> He'll take you to the finish, 'cause His love is stronger.

Amen to that.

## CHAPTER 3

# THE EMBRACING FATHER, PART I
## LUKE 15:11-24

Over the past several years, I have been associated with the ministry of night and day intercessory worship at the International House of Prayer in Kansas City. One of the focal points in that ministry has been to pray the apostolic prayers of the New Testament. Our rationale is that the apostolic prayers were inspired by the Holy Spirit as articulations of the will and purposes of God for the Body of Christ in every locale. Therefore, the full intent of Father God is to answer those prayers. One of the passages that is prayed most frequently is from Ephesians 1:17-23, where Paul the Apostle gives voice to a particular desire of the Spirit of God:

> . . . that the God of our Lord Jesus Christ, the Father of glory, may give to you the spirit of wisdom and revelation in the knowledge of Him, the eyes of your understanding being enlightened; that you may know what is the hope of His calling, what are the riches of the glory of His inheritance in the saints, and what is the exceeding greatness of His power toward us who believe, according to the working of His mighty power which He worked in Christ when He raised Him from the dead and seated Him at His right hand in the heavenly places, far above all principality and power and might and dominion, and every name that is named, not only in this age but also in that which is to come. And

**He put all things under His feet, and gave Him to be head over all things to the church, which is His body, the fullness of Him who fills all in all.**

This prayer has captured my heart, especially the phrase about the Father releasing a "spirit of wisdom and revelation in the knowledge of Him." What a wondrous concept to bring to the Lord in prayer! That God would reveal God to the human heart just because we ask Him to do so! As I've looked over journal entries and sermon notes from the past couple of decades, I have found that passage referenced time and again and have realized that the Lord has consistently reminded me to pray that prayer. He wants to reveal Himself to me and to anyone who will seek after Him! Holy Spirit, release to Your Bride in greater and greater measure this "spirit of wisdom and revelation" unto the knowledge of Christ and of the Father that He came to reveal so that our hearts may burn with the same love that we see to be in Him!

One of the most gripping portrayals of the Father that Jesus knew is found in Luke 15. Commonly known as "The Parable of the Prodigal Son," I prefer to call it "The Parable of the Embracing Father." It seems clear to me that Jesus' whole point in telling the story is to reveal the Father's heart to these two groups of people who are listening in rapt attention. I will make use of this chapter and the next in order to tell the story as fully as I can.

In this chapter, I want to focus particularly on the portion of the parable that deals with the younger son. I think this boy must have been the delight of his Father's heart. Bold and confident to the point of presumption, his approach to life is unconventional and daring. He is determined to have the fullest possible experience that will come to him.

Born with a gregarious personality, a typical second child, he is a people person, a natural leader. He is one who has grown up in a most favorable context yet without comprehending the blessing of his own environment. He is oblivious to the culture that the Father has built around him, a context in which the things of the Father are made easily accessible to the sons. As a matter of fact, the Father has established a motto in the home that is stated in the latter phrases of the parable: *"Son, you are always with me, and everything I have is yours."*

In this atmosphere of openness and generosity, the younger son has developed an open heart, a confidence, and strength of spirit that is exhilarating, even in its immaturity. He is doubtless the apple of the Father's eye, and he intends to take advantage of that fact. This intent has been stimulated by the imaginations of his mind, for he has begun to think about the far country. The far country here represents not so much physical distance from the Father's presence but an emotional and spiritual gap that has grown up in the son's heart as he has given himself to foolish imaginations. In his musings, he has made room for the voice of the Seductress, the Siren who sings her song to his heart. She has begun to convince him that in order to find the emotional, spiritual, and relational fulfillment that he longs for, he must leave the Father's house.

## Missing the Father's Heart

What this reveals to us is that the younger son did not really know his Father's heart. As we will come to see, and as Jesus revealed in the first two parables of Luke 15, this Father is a celebrating, joyful party animal! He'll throw a party for seemingly no reason at all! He is filled with joy when the things He designed for His own pleasure are restored to His house. He is quick to invite all the neighbors and have a party, celebrating whatever needs to be celebrated. "I found a sheep! Quick, let's have a party!" Or, "Hey, I found the coin I lost – put the shrimp on the barby and let's have some fun!" But the younger son, in the place of his daydreaming, had been lied to. His choice was to believe the lie that if he was going to live with freedom and celebration, he was going to have to find it somewhere else. So, he hatches a plan.

The text of Luke 15:12 tells us that the younger son came to the Father to ask for his portion of the inheritance. From one perspective, this is simply an expression of what the Father has obviously cultivated. He has fostered a strong spirit in his son, confident and assuming that the Father would be glad to share His wealth with His sons. According to current custom, however, this request was brazen and cold, inconsiderate of protocol, and deeply dishonoring to his Father. In that culture, the inheritance was divided among the heirs on the occasion of the death of the Father, and even then, the older son would have received his portion first. The older son's share would be a double portion, and the younger son would have normally been content to receive his smaller part in the proper time.

This boy does not approach the situation in that way. He comes boldly into the Father's presence to make his request. He has been nurtured beyond his own comprehension in the environment of the Father's love. In his immature presumption, he is delightful to the Father, even though his request will be a grievous one: "Father, give me the portion of goods that falls to me." It sounds rather innocuous on the surface, but lurking underneath are all the unspoken desires of license, lack of wisdom, and lack of restraint. I believe that the Father perceives all these underground realities, and though he does not address them, his heart is broken by the spiritual distance that has just been exposed.

The son is basically saying to the Father, "I know there is an inheritance coming, but I can't wait around for you to die and release it. It's taking too long, and I have places to go, people to meet, and things to do!" It's a daring and unthinkable request, one totally out of sync with the relational boundary lines of the day. No doubt, the older son hears of the request and is properly offended. The older brother assumes his offense is for the sake of the Father, but the Father is not grieved for himself but for his foolish son.

The Father's response is consistent with the motto of the home – "everything I have is yours." So even though there was no possible arena of need for the younger son unless he was planning to leave, the Father divided up the inheritance between them. He fully knows that the boy will be vacating his room within a short time. This is one of the realities that I believe the Holy Spirit desires for us to understand about the heart of the Father. Everything He has is ours, it is for our benefit, and it is available to us now, even in the context of our immaturity. It is His desire that we would receive His bounty with gratitude and live in our inheritance in a place of intimate relationship with Him. However, He understands that sometimes it is necessary to let us go our own way for a season.

## A Revelation of Generosity

I had a dream some years ago which the Lord used to speak to me very deeply. It was a dream in which I found myself flying in an airplane around the coastline of Monte Carlo. The scene was breathtakingly beautiful, and I could see the palace in the background where the Monarch of Monaco, Prince Rainier, had his dwelling. Suddenly the scene changed, and I was driving up to the palace gates. In the dream, I have the understanding that I am going to meet with Prince Rainier. I am driving an old clunker car, and as I come to the gates of the palace, the gates swing open. I drive into the courtyard of the palace and realize that I am dressed as I am normally dressed, in blue jeans and a golf shirt.

As I get out of the car and begin to walk up into the palace grounds, the Prince is walking down to meet me. I have brought a little gift for him, and all of a sudden, as I am walking to meet the Prince, I realize my condition. I look back to my car, sort of in the hope that I can go back and escape, but the servants have already taken my car. In fact, there is another car in its place, a new car, far more valuable and luxurious than the one I came in. As I walk up toward the Prince, I am suddenly conscious of how I am dressed, and I realize the absurdity of bringing this little gift to the Prince. I want to retreat, but it is now too late, and I am stuck in this situation. So I walk forward, and the Prince comes to me and I make some feeble attempt to greet him. What do I say here? As I make an awkward attempt to greet him and introduce myself, he says, "I know who you are, Gary; welcome here." He graciously accepts my gift and then he takes me on a personal tour around the palace grounds with his arm around my back. At the close of the dream, he said, "Gary, welcome to my kingdom; everything I have is at your disposal." The dream ended and I woke up.

Many years later, this dream is still a photograph in my mind. What was being communicated to me in an embryonic way was the truth of the heart of my Father saying to me as His child, "everything I have is yours – everything!" Over the years, the Lord has affirmed that to me again and again, and it is foundational to our confidence in Him to understand that His heart is open toward us even in our places of immaturity and lack of wisdom. Many believers would have this in their theology, but that theology is just two-dimensional and black-and-white. There is a need for us to know in the three-dimensional, color reality of our experience that the Father will not withhold anything from us.

Let's get back to the parable. It's not long before the younger son does the predictable thing. He takes his portion of the inheritance and heads off for the far country, where he is going to test his independence and look for all the fun promised him in his imagination. There are several key things of which he is unaware as he leaves the Father's house. This young boy is unaware that all of his confidence and strength has been nurtured in the environment of his Father's love and approval. The atmosphere of freedom and liberty has been normal for him, but he is not aware that this atmosphere is not normal in the far country. He has been plugged into the Father's life much more deeply than he realizes, and as he leaves, he is unaware that his umbilical cord is dragging along on the ground behind him, disconnected from all that gave him life.

### Created for Intimacy with God

God has created us to be receivers of the life that is poured out from His presence into our hearts. We were not created to live independently; we need nourishment from outside ourselves and can only thrive when we are joined to a vibrant and healthy life-source. This life-source for every person is our Father God, whether we believe in Him or not. We are created to live and move in Him, to have our existence in Him, to have all our fountains in Him. We cannot exist on our own, and if we are not rooted and grounded in His love, we will find some substitute source in which to plug in, to the ruination of our souls.

You see, every one of us was created to be joined with the Father, to be one with Him and to have His Spirit vibrate within us. We were designed to have His love and life-flow course through our veins, and so as we read through the Scriptures we see various analogies that speak of these things. For example, we read about living water, when Moses struck the rock in the Old Testament. The water gushed forth, and the people received life from drinking water from the Father's hand. We know from the New Testament that this Rock was none other than Jesus Himself.[1]

The analogy of the vine and the branches that we see in John 15 is powerful. The branch is joined with the vine in an essential way so that the life-flow comes through the vine and into the branches. There is a union, a oneness, and a drawing of life from the connection there. So all through the Scripture there is this analogy of life being drawn from –in a sense being drunk from – those with whom we are in relationship.

Jesus is telling this story as the true Son of the Father, who had left His Father's home to come to the far country of the created world. However, He came in the reality of intimacy with the Father and in the fullness of the Father's timing. Therefore, He came with all His heart connections with the Father fully intact and thus would not be dissipated by encounters with broken people. But the younger son was not in that place of intimacy or

---

[1] See *1 Corinthians 10:4*

right timing. His venture was premature, not motivated by intimate communion with the Father, but by carnal curiosity, and he
lived it to the fullest. The text says, "he wasted his possessions
with prodigal living."

"Prodigal" here means lavish, wastefully extravagant. He
spent it all, and the people in the far country were all too glad to
take it from him. This poor young boy had no idea what he was
getting into. He did not realize that he was seen as nothing but
fresh meat for a consumptive culture, one in which relationships
were not for nurturing but for consuming. He had entered the
world of broken people who were disconnected from any source
of life. The people in the far country were looking for someone to
whom they could connect in a vain and self-centered attempt to
satisfy the longings in their own souls. At first, he was happy to
comply, for his pockets were full and his spirit was free. He was
full of the residue of openness and confidence he carried with
him from the Father's house. He was generous of spirit because
he had been nurtured in that kind of environment, but he was ill-
prepared for the voracious appetites of the party-world he was
engaging.

Because he was premature in his venture and had left intimacy behind him, the shallowness of his resource began to be
apparent in short order. He was no longer connected to the deep
emotional wells of his Father's house. He could no longer sit at
the Father's table and simply bask in the presence of unconditional love and affirmation. Leaving the Father's open world of
"everything I have is yours" and entering the black-hole world of
"I have nothing, but whatever you have I'll take" soon did him
in. Before long, he had spent all he had in wild living, and he
began to be in want.

The dynamic here is that the branch has been separated from
the vine and has become grafted into another kind of vine. The
branch has joined itself to an unwholesome tree, and the young
son finds himself in a desperate place. He finds himself thirsty
and broken because the dynamic of life is that whomever and
whatever we join ourselves to, we draw life from that reality.

Those of you who have ever been in love have known this reality. I have been married thirty-one years at the time of this writing, and I will tell you that my wife Mary is a fountain of life to me. I remember when I first started going out with her, there was something happening in my heart so that whenever I saw her or heard her voice on the phone, things just kind of got all shaky on the inside! There was a drawing from her spirit because I saw in my wife somebody that I wanted to attach to and draw from. There was a union that was happening in our spirits and later on when we were married, happened in our flesh, and over the years, it has continued to grow. We became a channel of the Father's energy and life to one another. This is how the Father has created us, and when we are in healthy relationships, we are strengthened in them.

This young man was experiencing the opposite of this positive reality. He became overwhelmed with brokenness because as he went to the far country, the people with whom he entered into intimacy were fractured souls. They were broken people that did not know how to give but only knew how to take, people whose spirits were polluted. When he joined himself to them, he became polluted as well. He drank the water of brokenness, the water of slavery. What became the experience of his inner spirit eventually became the condition of his outer life, and he lost his sense of sonship. He became one for whom nobody cared, one who sold himself as a slave to the world.

Many of us know this person, don't we? Many of us have been this person, trying to draw life from hearts that are shattered. We have been trying to find that exhilaration of spirit, that exuberance of life that only comes from one place, the heart of Father God. We have known people and have been people who have drawn from illicit sexual relationships and have reaped the deadly consequences in our bodies and in our souls. This is why fornication and adultery is such a deadly thing. It is not that God is against sensual fulfillment. I want to tell you that God is for sensual fulfillment! He created it, and it is an integral part of the exhilaration of the marriage relationship. When a husband and wife come into oneness, they experience the joy of the Lord together and the blessing of the Holy Spirit is on their marriage. As they come into union sexually and physically, emotionally and spiritually, there is a drawing of life, an exhilaration of spirit that is right and good. As they share their whole being together, they are lifted up into the very presence of God. They are empowered to touch the human joy that is the closest thing to the eternal bliss of intimacy with Jesus, which is the whole point of our existence.

When the byproducts of holy intimacy are made the goal, people begin to break. The young son in our story focused on the byproducts of relationships and made them his goal. Therefore, the only people with whom he could interact were those who were broken and fractured in their own experience. So as he joined with them, he drank from them not life but death, not fulfillment but despair, not freedom but bondage and slavery.

It is not only in sexual relationships that this happens. It happens every time we join ourselves to someone or something other than the Father to find our significance and our worth. Every time we look to our external relationships, to a job opportunity, or to a certain level of income, we set ourselves up for brokenness. Every time we look to a church structure, to anything but the Father as our ultimate source of drawing life, we end up fractured. Do you see? This is so because it is only His life that brings us what we need and what we want. It is only His life that is whole.

## Hanging Out in Wholeness

I had a conversation with my son David some years ago that was very telling to me. I was talking with him at dinner one night when he was ten and in the fourth grade. He was talking about his day's activities at school, and I said, "David, who are you hanging out with?" He immediately replied by saying, "Dad, I'm not hanging out with anybody!" Now I can remember when I was ten and all of these feelings came upon me like a flood! Is my son being rejected? Is he lonely? I'm going through all this stuff in my mind, but I was cool on the outside. I said to him, "You're not hanging out with anybody?" And then Dave said a profound thing to me. I'm still blown away by it all these years later. He said, "Dad, hanging out means that you start to think and act like them, and I am not hanging out with anybody!" I was just stunned! So after I regained my composure, I said, "Well, who is hanging out with you?", and he named about five kids!

The spirit of God spoke to my heart and reminded me of a text from John 2:23-25, where it says this:

**While He was in Jerusalem at the Passover feast, many people saw the miraculous signs He was doing and believed in His name, but Jesus would not entrust Himself to them, for He knew all men and He did not need man's testimony about man, for He knew what was in a man.**

I was always puzzled by the phrase "Jesus would not entrust Himself to them" because it seemed to imply that Jesus was invulnerable to people. But that is not the truth. Jesus was vulnerable, He showed His disciples everything about Himself, He came vulnerably. The disciples were the ones He told about His experience in the wilderness, about His temptation. He let them watch Him in the Garden of Gethsemane – He was vulnerable. Jesus, what did you mean you never entrusted yourself? And the Lord explained that text to me through my son in that conversation. "What that means is that my Son came into the world whole because of His relationship with me," the Father said. "He drew His life, His identity, His purpose from me and looked to no other source to meet His need. Jesus looked to no other source to identify Himself, looked to no other Spirit but my Spirit to gain life."

Do you see what He is saying? He entrusted himself to no one but the Father for His identity and liberty. That made Him free to be the one that people "hung out" with. The dynamic of walking in the power and the joy of the Christian life is not to be "hangers out," but to be those around whom other people hang out. That is what the Father has for us. We are not to be those who go into the world like the younger son looking for a place to belong, a nipple to latch onto, an outlet to plug into. This young boy had gone into the far country with his umbilical cord in his hand, saying, "Where do I plug in? Oh, that's not it, try again!" I am telling you that there is only one place the plug fits, and that is in the heart of the Father. We are to draw life from Him, not from anything else, not from anyone else. Let the ears of your heart hear this teaching!

So, the young man in our story finds himself in a big pile of trouble. Then, to top it all off, God sends a famine in the land! Do we understand that God is quite willing to orchestrate our own personal little crisis moment so that we will experience our depth of need and return to His heart? Up to this point, the son has only "begun to be in need," but now the need intensifies. He is not yet to the place of true humility and despair, so he still thinks he has what it takes to survive in the far country. He'll just get a good job, and everything will be fine!

However, because of the famine, good jobs are next to impossible to find. After much searching, he finds himself in the employ of a pig farmer, who sends him out to feed the pigs. Now, it doesn't take much understanding to see the focused irony of Jesus' teaching here. For a good Jewish boy, the idea of a job feeding pigs is as low as it can go. Pigs were unclean; they were seen as symbolic of demonic activity, and Jesus' point is that the son had reached the bottom of barrel in his search for survival. What was worse, the only food available was the food the pigs ate, and he was not even permitted to eat that! No one gave him anything.

### Coming to His Senses

So the son has come to a point of slavery, a pit of despair. He recognizes that he has lost his sense of sonship, and he no longer feels worthy to be a son. How many do you know who are there? Do you find yourself in this place? At this point, the son only has one thing going for him. The biblical text declares that "he came to his senses." He knew enough about his Father to know that he could go home, if not as a son, then as a slave. The son began to realize that because of his experience in the world, it is better to be a servant of the Father then a son of the world. He then started home, and he had his speech all prepared. Have you ever prepared a speech for God? What you are going to say when you finally come around to asking forgiveness one more time? This boy was all prepared with his speech, and now I want you to see the Father.

The Father in His wisdom has let the boy go. He has let this son come to the full experience of his desperation. Did the Father send the trouble? Mostly not, for the world has trouble enough of its own, and God often does not need to send anymore. However, there are times when, due to rebellion and hardness of heart, the Father does send trouble, and so I suggest that the Father was involved in the famine that came into the land. The circumstance God allowed magnified the difficulty that the boy was experiencing. Some of us have plugged into all the wrong outlets, and then we wonder how come God sends us trouble all the time. God doesn't need to send trouble to most of us. Most of us have created enough trouble of our own, and our difficulties are simply the matter of reaping the fruit of the sowing we have done. God simply waits patiently for us to grow weary of sleeping in the bed we have made. Now, if we become stubborn and refuse to respond to the corrective wooing of the Holy Spirit, the Father is quite willing to orchestrate our own personal famine. He doesn't hesitate in doing this so that we'll get real hungry and thirsty. That's what has happened in our story.

So the boy goes home. You can imagine the heaviness of his steps as he nears the Father's estate, all the while rehearsing the speech. Imagine the agony of heart that he is experiencing, the questions and tension, when all of a sudden, here comes the Father! He has been watching from the entrance to the estate for

months. He sees the boy come, and He runs out. In that culture,
it was definitely not proper for a respected man to run in public,
but this Father does not care! He picks up the skirts of His robe
and hurries down the road to meet His boy! He embraces the
boy, and I love the force of the original language: "The Father
simply could not stop kissing His son!" He sees His son, this
fractured, enslaved son walking home, and the Father comes and
embraces him. He kisses him, takes His son back into His bosom,
and says, "Now just drink, just drink, just let me hold you, boy,
you are so tired!" Can you feel His heart? There is no scolding,
there is no condemnation, no "I told you so." He does not ask the
boy what he did with all the money. There is only an understanding, a knowledge that this kid tried to find a plug-in that did not
fit. The Father responds so gently and compassionately in view of
His son's anguish: "Come, come on, give yourself to me, plug in
here, drink from me. Let the life of my Spirit flow back into you,
let sonship be restored, right now, let your slavery fall off, let it
go." That is the Father that Jesus knew.

The son actually is so unprepared for this kind of reception
that he pushes himself away from the Father in order to go
through his speech. He has been practicing this thing all the way
home: "Father, I have sinned against heaven and against You." So
far, so good. He is accurate in this confession, and the Father
allows him to voice his godly sorrow. But then the boy tries to go
into the second part of the speech: "I am no longer worthy to be
called your son . . . ." But before he can get to the part about
making him a hired servant, the Father interrupts him. You can
almost imagine Him clapping His hand over His son's mouth
and saying, "Stop talking like that. In your brokenness, do not
presume to understand my heart for you. Servants, my son is
home! Bring the robes, bring the ring, bring the shoes, and restore
my son to his rightful place. Not only that, but kill the fatted calf;
we are going to have a party!"

The robe is a picture of family identity. By giving the son his
robe, the Father was once again acknowledging that this boy
belonged to him. The ring was the symbol of authority, and the

Father was declaring that this wasteful son still had full access to all the Father's resources. Shoes were a symbol of sonship and meant that this boy had the right to walk around everything that belongs to his Father and claim it as his own. When people exchanged property in biblical times, they presented each other a pair of shoes that they might put on the shoes and go out and walk around the property, possessing their kingdom. So the son comes home, and the Father breaks out the robe, the ring, and the sandals and clothes his son again. In that one action, He says to His son "Slave? Never, never! You are my son; you belong here, and everything I have is yours!" Do you see it? And they began to celebrate.

We are scandalized by the profligate mercy of the Father. The true prodigal in the story is the Father. He is filled with lavish and extravagant mercy that shatters the boundaries of our expectations and breaks the icons of false images of God that keep us at a distance from His heart. We say, "Where is the accountability?" The fact is there was great accountability, established in the assignments to the servants to dress the son. They are being commanded to stay with him, to ensure his understanding of his sonship, for they know that he will live out of his self-perception. He may forget from time to time and begin to regress into worldly attitudes. After all, he got a little brain damaged out there. But the Father is so confident in the power of His love and the ministry of His servants that He doesn't even bother with a probationary period. He simply restores the boy. Period.

I remember a time like this in my own life. I had spent the first part of one summer touring with a music group from the Christian college that I attended. I was 19 years old, experiencing my first extended ministry trip. I had no idea of the physical, emotional, and spiritual backlash that would come after seven weeks of travel and performance. Being too poor to afford to go to my parents' home for the remaining six weeks of summer, I got a job with a construction crew and proceeded to live out the summer in foolish dissipation – drinking beer, playing softball, and generally being stupid. Probably the only reason that I didn't get into real trouble was that real trouble was hard to find in the little Mennonite community in which my college was located.

I found out many years later that the college president and some of the board members were keenly aware of my behavior. Because I had been representing the college, they were considering asking me not to return to school. I was in the far country of my own foolishness, needing the Father's heart, but having no idea how to find it.

The time came for school to begin again, and on registration day, I found myself walking toward the library building to complete one aspect of registration. As I proceeded down the sidewalk, I noticed a man walking toward me. It was Dr. Prieb, the English professor and Dean of the college. He was a very godly and kind man, but that day he was the last person I wanted to encounter. He represented everything that I had dishonored in my foolishness, and I wanted to avoid him at all costs.

I moved to the side of the walkway, only to see him move in front of me. I shifted to the other side; he moved in front of me again, and I realized that he meant to meet me head on. I was embarrassed, ashamed, with nothing to say. Dr. Prieb had every right to chew me out, to reprimand me, and demand restitution for the embarrassment I had brought to the school.

As we met, something entirely unexpected happened. He stood before me, extended his arms around me, and drew me to himself. I was completely stiff and unresponsive, having no grid for what was happening. As he drew me near, this man who knew the Father's heart whispered in my ear "Welcome home, Gary." Then he kissed me on the cheek, and let me go. I was stunned. This was totally out of my paradigm. I deserved rebuke and dismissal, and received mercy and grace. I will never forget that day, and I will never forget that man.

The issue is this: Is this the Father you know? This is the Father we have, but sometimes it is difficult to see Him accurately. Our hearts have been clouded by bad models and by the desire to plug in to places that cannot feed us the life we crave, but only feed us death.

Jesus told this story to the Pharisees and to the tax collectors and sinners that they might know the truth of the Father's identity. The teaching came from the one Son who drew His life only from the Father. It shook their perceptions to the core, and it should do the same to ours. I tell you if you do not know a Heavenly Father like this one, you have not been plugged in to the right place. If this is not the God you know, you don't know God, because this is His heart. I don't mean that you are not saved or not going to heaven when you die. It does mean that you have not yet had the eyes of your heart enlightened to know the precious reality of your Father's character and your identity as His son or daughter. My prayer as you continue through this book is that you would come to know the Father Jesus knew and that your heart will be captured as mine has been by His tender mercies and His great affection for you.

## CHAPTER 4

# THE EMBRACING FATHER, PART II
## LUKE 15:25-32

When Jesus came to the earth and began to minister to the people of first century Palestine, His declared purpose was that the nature and character of God would be revealed to their hearts. The religious systems of that time had so distorted the truth of God's identity as a passionate Father that He was virtually unknowable. Only a very few individuals, people like Anna and Simeon,[1] had found the grace to look past all the structured religion and discover the true reality of this beautiful and passionate God. Jesus came to change that reality, to invite people into a new and dynamic relationship with a passionate and tender Father, whose character and personality was perfectly represented by His faithful Servant Son.

Some years ago, when I was pastoring within the Vineyard network of churches, John Wimber, the leader of the Vineyard network at that time, was teaching about the function of the Law of God in relationship to His people. In order to communicate his understanding of this, John shared a word-picture that has stayed with me over time. The picture is of a mother carrying an infant child who is bound to her by one of those contraptions that we called "Snugglies" when my kids were small. A "snuggly" is a

---

[1] See *Luke 2:25-38*

system of pouches and straps that carries the child on the parent's chest so that there is nearness and yet freedom. The purpose of the "snuggly" is to facilitate closeness and intimacy, but in itself, it is nothing but a structure of cloth and metal fasteners. There is no life in the "snuggly." It exists solely to bind the child to the one who has the life.

Wimber's suggestion was that this was the intent of God as He gave the Law and allowed the development of the religious practices of the day. Because the Holy Spirit would not be poured out in a general way until the Day of Pentecost, the Law of God was still external. Therefore, there was need for an external system of practices that would facilitate intimacy, holding the children near to the Father's heart. This needed to be in place until the coming of Jesus and the release of the Holy Spirit would write the Law on their hearts and faith would become internalized. In other words, the Law and the practices of Jewish religion were to be a kind of "snuggly" for the soul. God never intended for the performance of the religious externals to become the point. That would be like a child trying to eat the "snuggly" instead of drinking life from the mother's breast. There is no nourishment there; it is strictly functional.

### Intimacy and Task-Orientation

Now, if you combine this reality with the fact that a substantial portion of created humanity has been designed by the Father to be task-oriented (do we understand that the Father is *seriously* task-oriented?), you have a true opportunity for massive disaster. Remember, the purpose of the Father's heart is intimacy, and even the fulfilling of task is to be in the context of intimate partnership. The structures of the religious system were given to facilitate intimacy until faith was released[2] but were never intended to be a substitute for intimacy. However, if you combine a system of external practices with task-oriented people who are fallen

---

[2] See *Galatians 3:22-25*

and broken, you have set the stage for religious performance. This performance orientation can move quickly away from the intimacy that was the goal from the beginning. Then, if on top of all of that, you add the reality of human honor and deference given to those who perform better than anyone else, there can quickly emerge a hierarchy of the "haves and have-nots." These are people who are seen to be successful in the task in comparison with those who are failures.

It is this conglomeration of people that are gathered to hear Jesus as He tells the stories recorded in Luke 15. Here He stands as the Son of God who does all the Father's will. Yet He does it with such pleasure and grace, such gladness of heart that the religious leaders are stunned and put off. On the other hand, the "have-nots" – those who have become disenfranchised by the system – receive Him with delight and enjoyment. This man is modeling the kind of life they always wanted, a life of happy holiness and fervency. Jesus is addressing both groups in turn. He has just finished speaking to those who have left the Father's house because of boredom and a carnal desire for adventure and who have become broken and dissipated in the process. He has welcomed them back into the Father's presence with such mercy and tenderness that they are staggered at the scope of the invitation.

And now, the faithful Son turns His attention to the other group. These are the older sons who have remained in the Father's house but who are about to be exposed as just as distant from the Father's heart as the younger son ever was. It is so important that we understand the motivation of Jesus' heart as He speaks these impacting things to the scribes and Pharisees. His heart is filled with desire for them. He loves them deeply and addresses them as sons of the Father. They are His brothers, estranged though they may be. As He begins to relate the story of the older brother, the heart of the embracing Father longs to draw these men back to His breast. Jesus longs to bring them near so that they might once again drink the water of life on which they were designed to live.

Some time ago the Lord spoke to me through John 14:23 –

**If anyone loves Me, he will keep My Word; and my Father will love him, and We will come to him and make Our home with him.**

I believe that in a powerful way the Father is revealing Himself to His Church in the depth of His identity as Father. For many years, we have not known who the Father is in an accurate way. We have had strong emphases on doctrinal purity, but it has only served to lead us to massive division and sectarianism. We have had a good understanding of what it means to become a Christian in the terms that will lead us to heaven when we die, but that understanding has been reduced to a few statements of mental assent and a rote prayer. We have built all sorts of self-help programs to deal with our sin patterns, but the Body of Christ is rife with brokenness and unrepentant sin. We have had leadership conferences stacked on top of leadership conferences, and there is still massive crisis at every level of Church leadership. Our pastors are caught in patterns of aggressive striving, competition, jealousy toward other ministries, and outright sin. We have emphasized missions and the extension of the Kingdom of God, but our missionaries are burning out at record rates and leaving the mission fields faster than we can replace them. Where we have mostly succeeded is in building buildings, but we have not come to learn who God is very well. The wine of contemporary Christian faith is old, and the wineskins are dried up and brittle. We desperately need a new perspective of who God is and what He is about in order to be about His business in an effective way. I believe that Jesus is standing in our midst again, desiring to show us the Father, and it is necessary for us all to humble our hearts that we may see His glory, His love, and His power.

So once again, the Father is going to disclose Himself to the people of that time and through this story, to us. In the second part of the story of the embracing Father, Jesus turns his attention to the men who made up the leadership of the broken and ineffective system of that day, even as He speaks to us today about our condition as older sons.

When the younger son came to the Father and asked for his share of the inheritance, his Father said, "Sure, take what is yours!" knowing full well that the son was going to blow it. I believe He knew what was about to transpire. Dads are not dumb, especially this dad. The boy headed out into the world, blew it, and came back home with his tail between his legs. He came crying out for bare mercy, not knowing that the Father had been praying and planning for his return. The boy asked for a job and got full restoration. He got full love, got the shoes put back on His feet, got restored back to the fullness of relationship and sonship. He was set in a context where he could be healed, and then they had a celebration, a big party and killed the fatted calf.

But even as the Father is celebrating the joy of the restored life of His wayward son, we encounter another member of the family whom most of us know very well. Most of us knew the first son pretty well, and most of us know the second son pretty well. You see, a little bit of both boys lives in each of us, doesn't it? As matter of fact, I find that the longer the prodigal stays at home, the greater the danger is that he will become like the older brother. The longer the children who were once wayward stay in the Father's house, the harder it is for them to give grace to those who are coming in at entry level, unless they stay intimately connected to the Father's heart. This older brother had not stayed connected, and so what we have here is one who has been around for awhile, who has been hanging out at the Father's house without touching the Father's heart. The story goes like this:

**Meanwhile, the older son was in the field, and when He came near the house He heard music and dancing and He called one of His servants and asked Him what was going on. "Your brother's come," they replied, "and your Father has killed the fattened calf because He has him back safe and sound." The older brother became angry and refused to go in, so His father went out and pleaded with him, but he answered his Father saying "all these years I have been slaving for you, and I have never disobeyed your orders,**

**yet you never gave me even a young goat so I could cele-
brate with my friends, but when this son of yours has
squandered your property with prostitutes comes home,
you kill the fatted calf for him." "My son," the father said,
"you are always with me and everything I have is yours. We
had to celebrate and be glad because this brother of yours
was dead and is alive again, He was lost and now He is
found." (Luke 15:25-32)**

The older son is out working in the field, doing what he has
always done. He's a responsible, industrious guy, just taking care
of business as he knew business should be taken care of. After all,
he knew that what the Father had said all along was true. He had
read Deuteronomy 27:17 and knew that the inheritance was coming to him. He knew that if he was faithful and obedient and
stayed around home that eventually when the old man died he
was going to get most of it. The younger brother had already
been given his portion, and the older son was operating in the
self-satisfaction of never having questioned his Father's orders.

The problem was that this son did not understand the true
nature of his inheritance. He was under the impression that the
most valuable thing that was coming to him was the estate, when
in fact he was created not primarily for ownership but for relationship. The Father's deepest desire has always been to have
intimate relationship with His sons. The issues of estate, property,
and activity have always been secondary in His heart. I do not
mean that the task is insignificant. I mean to say that in the heart
of God, the pursuit of the task has always been a means to an
end, and that end is intimate relationship with Him.

It has already been established elsewhere that the highest
place of destiny in our lives is intimacy with God as our Father
and with His Son Jesus Christ as our beloved Bridegroom. The
culmination of the ages is the Wedding Supper of the Lamb,
when Jesus and His Bride are fully joined together in the glory of
His presence. In the light of that destiny, we are told in Ephesians
2:10 that we are God's workmanship,

**Created in Christ Jesus for good works, which God
prepared beforehand that we should walk in them.**

The picture that helps me understand this reality is this: I
believe that in Christ, all of the facets of the character of the
Father are fully expressed. Having been chosen in Christ from the
foundations of the world,[3] every individual has been fashioned
by God around a particular facet of His being. We have each been
specifically prepared for good works, the things God wants to
accomplish on the earth. He doesn't need help for these things –
He is the Creator of the universe! Rather, He wants to do them in
partnership with people He loves. In His wisdom, He places a
sense of destiny and purpose in the heart of every individual, but
He only releases to them a portion of the whole thing. Because
His ultimate goal is intimacy with us, the Father hides a significant part of our identity and destiny in His own heart. This is so
that the fullness of it cannot be realized apart from Him. Proverbs
25:2 tells us that part of God's glory is that He conceals things,
and that part of the glory of kings is to search out that which is
concealed.

When God hides the fullness of our identity and destiny in
His heart, He does it for the sake of His glory and ours. He does
not do this because He is closed to us, but precisely to draw us to
Himself. The drive to know our destiny is in reality a drive to
know Him, for it is only in intimacy with Him that we can find
the fullness of our own being. The dilemma is that in our place of
brokenness, with our intimacy interrupted by sin, we assume that
this partial awareness of purpose and destiny is a job description.
We think it's a blueprint for tasks to perform so that we might
receive the Father's approval and, at the end of the day, find intimacy as the reward of our labors. The point of frustration for us
is that we can't seem to find the keys to the closet that contains
this job description!

---

[3] See *Ephesians 1:4*

## Intimacy is the Root-System of Labor

But intimacy is not the reward of our labors! It is the root-system out of which our labors are to proceed! Jesus, the true Son, declared that it was precisely because the Father loved Him that He showed Jesus all that He was doing, so that Jesus might do it with Him.[4] Jesus never worked *for* the Father; He always and only worked *with* the Father in the context of intimate relationship.

This is the dilemma that so often faces those who are created as task-oriented people. We receive a sense of what God desires to do with us, and we take it as a job description, something to produce for God out of our own resources. From this perspective, our very sense of personal worth is dependent upon the successful completion of the task. Therefore, resources must be gathered and focused upon the accomplishment of the task. People become resource units, not brothers and sisters in the family. Labor consumes us instead of refreshing us. Apart from intimacy with the Father, the job soon becomes slavery, and joyful partnership gives way to bitter self-serving. It is a tragic misunderstanding of God's intent.

The older brother was completely caught in this dilemma. He had completely missed the heart of the Father and was fully severed from any place of intimacy. He had no sense of partnership with the Father, no sense of being settled in an inheritance of the heart. So, he was out in the field, not tending His father's property, but *his* property. He was taking care of his business, making sure that it stayed in good repair for the time that would come when he would inherit it. The older son was working hard, being industrious, and being a good citizen. He would make it well in our society today. He knew what it was to put in an honest day's work. It was not a question of overtime; it was the matter of spending whatever time the task required. He knew what it was to be an achiever, an overachiever.

---

[4] See *John 5:19-20*

Somewhere along the way, this son had decided that in order for him to come into his inheritance he had to go out and make it happen. He became a workaholic, a performer, one who was dedicated to doing well enough to earn the Father's inheritance. He had given up on knowing the Father's pleasure; to him, that was an inconceivable thing. There was no joy in his life, only the pursuit of some distant inheritance. It was a pursuit that left him bitter and enslaved, separated from his true destiny of intimacy with the Father, and filled with resentment and ill will.

Somebody said one time that people need to be able to say three things: "yes," "no," and "whoopee!" This son had no "whoopee" in his life. This is a boring guy. He is bored and angry, and he is determined that no one else is going to have any fun either. Therefore, we can only imagine what is going on in his mind as he comes home from the field one day to hear the music of celebration coming from the house.

This guy doesn't like celebration. Having a party just seems frivolous to him. Surely it has driven him crazy to come in from time to time only to find a party going on because some sheep has been found or some lost trinket recovered. So the brother comes home. He hears this music going, and his first response is "what now?" He grabs the first servant he can find and asks, "What is the meaning of all this?"

I imagine that the servant is caught up in the celebration. He is deeply enjoying it because he knows the Father's heart better than the son does. But now this servant has a problem. The older brother is his boss, his foreman, and so he has to explain it to him. I can imagine that at first he spills over with the excitement of the event and says, "Oh, man, are we having a party today! Your brother has come home, and the Father is overjoyed, so much so that He has ordered the fatted calf to be killed! All the neighbors are coming, and the party is on!"

The older brother is indignant, filled with rage, and storms away from the place, refusing to come into the party. On one occasion, Jesus called the Pharisees "hypocrites" precisely for this reason. He said, *"You shut up the Kingdom of Heaven against men; you neither go in yourselves, nor do you allow those who are entering to go in"*(Matthew 23:13). He was saying to them, "Wake up, open your eyes, the kingdom has come, and it is a kingdom to be enjoyed!"

Remember that as Jesus was telling this story, it was in the context of having a dinner party with the tax collectors and sinners. These were the wayward ones who had come home to Jesus. They had come home to drink from His Spirit and to draw life from Him. He was the one they wanted to be with because they sensed wholeness in Him; they sensed reality in Jesus. They sensed that He actually liked them, that they could be around Him and not be condemned. They felt joyful and free in that setting, but the Pharisees and the teachers of the law were on the other side saying, "Shame on you for having fun!!"

## The Father's Open Heart

Notice the Father. Once again, the lavish love of the Father impels Him out of the house. For you see, the Father's heart is the same for both of His boys. The Father's heart is no different for the older brothers than it is for the wayward sons. So the Father leaves the celebration and goes out with no hint of judgment in His heart. He goes out to His older son and says, "Come on, come in! Don't you realize my son is back? Come in and celebrate with us!"

But the brother launches off into a tirade of hurt feelings and wounded emotions, and he begins a litany of self justification. He says, "Look, all these years I have been slaving for you!" He was not working for the Father; he was working for himself! "All of these years I have been slaving for you." Do you get the dynamic of what is happening here? He was just as far away from his Father as the younger son was! Even though he had stayed in the house, even though he had been in the proximity of the Father, he was in a far country in his heart. He had never experienced the joyfulness, the freedom, and the lavish love of his Father, even living under the same roof. He had decided that if anything was going to come to him, it was because he earned it and had it coming. He had done well enough, long enough, faithfully enough to get what he had coming.

The reason that we know that the older brother was in his own far country comes in verse 30. The text says:

**As soon as this son of yours came, who has devoured your livelihood with harlots, you killed the fatted calf for him.**

The interesting thing is that there is no other mention anywhere in the text of what the boy had done other than he had squandered his money in wild living. There is no mention of living with prostitutes at all except in the older brother's mind. It is a logical inference, but it is only an inference. You see, the dynamic that is going on is that while the younger brother was living out his fantasies, the older brother was repressing his and projecting them on the younger one. He had played the younger brother's tape over and over again in his mind and had judged him harshly. But he did not realize that he was as far from faithfulness to his Father as the younger brother was. The only difference was that he had stayed home. But he was broken in relationship, hindered in freedom, and did not know who his Father was.

It is a tragic thing to live close to the Father and not know who He is. It is a tragic thing to have a Father who is absolutely free, who is ready to celebrate, who is ready to embrace and wrestle and snuggle on the floor and not know Him. It is a tragedy to think that we have a performance-orientated Father when we don't. It is a tragedy to miss God like that, and most of us know this older brother because most of us are like him. We have missed the joy of our Father. We have wandered far in our minds, we have tried to find fulfillment in doing things for God. But the Father says, "O Beloved, don't you see, you have missed My heart? You could have had a party anytime! Don't you know that everything I have is yours?"

You see, what the older brother was saying was something

like this: "Father, it's okay for You to welcome him home; I understand Your willingness to take him back – but a party? Be serious! Why didn't You just honor his request and let him demonstrate his faithfulness now? A probationary time in the servants' quarters would have been good. But no, You are putting him right back on the pedestal! This is going too far! Forgiveness is fine, but restoration? Healing? Reinstatement of the inheritance?"

Can't you hear the voice of the Pharisee? What is it in his heart that tweaks him? What aggravates him to such a degree that he spews his frustration all over the Father? I believe it is the subconscious awareness of his own poverty of soul. He feels the emptiness of a broken relationship with the Father, and yet he is not willing to address it in real ways. Even as the older son is being invited into the celebration, he is accusing the Father of never making provision for a celebration for him. The sadness of this scene is overwhelming.

The Father's response to the older son is profound:

**"Son, you are always with me, and everything I have is yours. It was right that we should make merry and be glad, for your brother was dead and is alive again, and was lost and is found."**

In effect, the Father tells the son that he could have had a party any time he wanted one. He points out that the inheritance has always been available – indeed, it was divided between the boys right from the beginning of the story! The celebration was ongoing in the heart of the Father, and it was His desire that the older son live in that dynamic. The Father pleaded with the older son, but there was only a deaf ear. Jesus, ever the master storyteller, leaves the story hanging in the balance. He doesn't bring the story to an end; He leaves the older brother to make his own decision.

In this dramatic moment, Jesus is saying to the Pharisees, "Are you going to come in or not? Are you going to come to the party, or are you going to continue to refuse the knowledge of My heart? It is your choice, because you see, My heart is the heart of a celebrator. My heart is the heart of a free Father. My heart is one of restoration and wholeness, beauty, freedom, joy, healing, and wellness, and you have missed me." Beloved, wherever we are in our own lives, we need to see the Father's heart here. Whenever we think that anything we can do apart from His presence would improve our chances of the Father being pleased with us, we enter into the realm of the older brother. The Father's heart is the same for us as it is for these brothers: "Beloved, everything I have is yours! You're my son!"

There is something implicit in the story for which I am very grateful. It is that the younger brother did not encounter the older brother before he met the Father. Had it been the other way around, I wonder what would have happened? What would have happened to the coatless, shoeless, broken, and smelly kid if the Father had not been watching, and the older brother had met him first? He would never have made it home. One of the great points of sorrow in our day is that so very often when broken children desire to come back to Papa and to get healed up, they run into older brothers first. Many times, those older brothers look like us.

On the night that I first preached the message that is the foundation of this chapter, I pulled onto the freeway as I was driving to the Worship Center, and there was girl hitch hiking. I had an immediate sense that I was to pick her up. I found that she was just getting off from work, and I said asked her where she was headed. She said she was going to pay her bartender. She had apparently been so desperate for a drink that she had borrowed money from him. So I started talking with her and told her that I knew where she could get something good to drink. She responded with interest, so I invited her to come along to church to taste some "new wine," and to meet the Father. She responded that she had been to church and had had enough. I felt a deep grief in my spirit as I heard her response. She had never met the Father; instead, she had encountered older brothers. She had run into people who wanted to put upon her the things they have put upon themselves – that if we do the right thing long enough and faithfully enough, perhaps there will be a party when we get done. She had experienced the cold, small, joyless atmosphere of the older brother's influence, and it had caused her to miss the Lord.

On the other hand, just the other day I listened as one of the women who is a leader at the International House of Prayer in Kansas City was sharing a story. For years, the congregation that Rhonda and her husband Danny lead has gone down to one of the poorest sections of Kansas City to feed the homeless and celebrate with them in worship. They declare the goodness and kindness of God by ministering to the poor in practical ways. On a recent evening, as they were worshipping the Father on the streets, a man from the neighborhood came running up to them demanding to be led into salvation through Jesus. He wanted to be delivered from demons, baptized in water and the Holy Spirit, healed from physical problems – in short, he wanted the deluxe treatment of the Kingdom of God, all on that night. He was a man that was familiar in the neighborhood as an alcoholic, but as the group prayed for him that night, he was delivered and set free. In the aftermath of that encounter, one of the congregational members asked him about why he had waited so long, why he had come at this time.

His response was profound. He told the group that he had been watching for years as ministries would come and go, all with differing agendas. Cynicism had grown in his heart as he saw joyless, judgmental Christians trying to convert the people of the street without truly caring about them or even wanting to get to know them. So he had watched Rhonda and Danny's group for a long time. They came week after week, several nights a week, being with the people, sitting with them, praying for them, worshipping with them, and serving them with gladness of heart. Finally, he just couldn't take it any more. He saw the celebration, the glorious liberty of the sons of God, and he said, "I have to be like that." He came running to the Father's house, and he was received with gladness by servant-sons and daughters who know the Father's heart.

The Lord desires just such an atmosphere of celebration and liberty. He wants to release such a generosity of heart among His people that the broken will long to come in. They will recognize in the hearts of God's people the same heart that was in Jesus that made ruined people want to be near Him. He desires sons and daughters who will rejoice in the inheritance that is already theirs and that can be experienced today in the place of intimate affection. I remember a number of years ago when my son David was just learning how to talk, I was talking to him one afternoon, and I said, "David, what do you want to do tonight?" And he said, "I don't know, snuggle I think!" My heart was thrilled! Here was a child that knew what relationship with his father ought to be. I am convinced the Lord desires a houseful of sons and daughters like that, who know the heart of their Father and are delighted to celebrate His life together.

I believe that in this day, God is raising up a people that are determined to know this Father. These people want to know this generous and lively God who welcomes broken sons and daughters with kisses and gladness of heart. His desire is that performance-oriented sons and daughters would come to freedom and discover that their destiny is to be found only in the place of intimacy. The Father wants them to know that their lifework is to be lived out under an open heaven of revelation rooted in extravagant love. This Father is drawing the hearts of people everywhere into the place of prayer, declaring to them that intimacy with God is the fuel that drives their lives. We are discovering that He is indeed a good Father, and that He does in fact have wonderful things in store for those who will come to His presence with gratitude and joy.

The people of God are going to know the heart of God. His body is going to have His heart. It is not just that we will have good hearts; it is that we will have His heart. My question is this: what kind of heart beats within your breast? Is it the cold and stony heart of the older brother? If it is, I have wonderful news for you – there is a heart transplant available! God will take your heart of stone and give you a heart of flesh. He will put within us the passion that He carries within Himself. Jesus promised us that we would know the love of the Father to the fullest, and that the result for us would be fullness of joy. This is what we desire because He has placed that longing in our hearts. As we breathe back to Him His own will, He will surely give us what we ask.

## CHAPTER 5

# THE FORGIVING FATHER

MATTHEW 18:21-35

Perhaps one of the most potent, most familiar, and yet under-appreciated revelations in the Scripture is that God is a forgiving God. Forgiveness is one of those foundational teachings for the Body of Christ from the Scriptures that is absolutely fundamental to the faith. However, it has become so familiar that often believers have thoughts similar to this: "Well you know, forgiveness is important and all that, but I'm looking for something new and revelatory, on the cutting edge of what God is doing." Some years ago, when I was on the pastoral staff at Metro Christian Fellowship in Kansas City, I was asked to preach a series of messages on this topic, and I found myself thinking, "I'm sure I have some sermons in my files about the forgiveness of God. I'll sort of dust those off and refresh them with contemporary illustrations and simply reestablish that groundwork."

What happened to me was that I ran into a surprise. The Lord began to ambush me with a longing that was awakening in my own heart to know more and to understand more about His mercy and forgiveness. So as I prayed and contemplated the Word of God concerning forgiveness, I slowly became aware of a strange and disconcerting thing. I had a sense that something was enticing me and drawing me into a deeper level of understanding than I had known before. The bothersome thing was that it just stayed right on the edge of my vision and comprehension. I had this sweet and mysterious impression that I was about to discover something majestic. Perhaps you have had that kind of experience where it seems as though something or someone is speaking to you, drawing you, wooing you. It is as though the sound hangs just off to the side of your comprehension, and when you turn toward it, it keeps moving back away from your sight even as you are turning.

The best word picture that I was able to come up with concerning how I felt in the matter was this: I felt like a very small man in a very small boat with a few other people, sailing on a very small lake. Somehow, I had gotten the impression that there is an ocean somewhere. I had not seen the ocean except in the images of my mind. I had never smelled it, and I had never felt what it is to float in the majesty of that great sea, but I began to be convinced that it is there. On top of that, there began to come to me a longing to see that ocean, to plumb its depths. I wanted to cast myself adrift on it and entrust myself to its imposing swells. And now, with not nearly enough experience on that ocean, I have the responsibility of explaining it to you.

There is a wondrous passage in Psalm 130 that makes a powerful declaration about the forgiving nature of God. Verses three and four of that Psalm read this way:

**If You, LORD, should mark iniquities,
O Lord, who could stand?
But there is forgiveness with You,
That You may be feared.**

"If You should mark iniquities. . . ." The implication is that God, rather than being one who marks iniquities, is a God of forgiveness. His nature is to not hold on to grievances, but to send them away from people so that they might be re-established in mercy and grace. The Psalmist is so impacted by this realization that he insists it is a cause of the fear of the Lord being established in the hearts of human beings. As I consider the common response to the news that God forgives people, it seems that few people are moved to reverence and awe by this truth. Rather, most seem to sort of expect it and see that fact as license to continue to live as they want.

However, the way the text of the Psalm is ordered, it seems that the forgiving nature of God is something that ought to stimulate a holy fear. There should be a sense of sobriety and respect that comes in realizing that it is a stunning thing that God's nature and desire is to exercise forgiveness. My prayer is that as we consider this topic here, the Holy Spirit will release grace to us to experience wonderful joy in receiving forgiveness and also to know the life-changing power of holy fear as we consider that our Father is the Father of forgiveness.

I want to direct our attention to a powerful story, a parable of Jesus concerning forgiveness in God's Kingdom. Recorded in Matthew 18, the parable focuses three things: the awesome liberality of God's forgiveness, our tendency to settle for indebted slavery instead of free sonship, and finally, the torment of unforgiveness that God sometimes uses to drive us back to His mercy. Please take the time to read Matthew 18:21-35 before you proceed to the following paragraphs.

### God's Liberal Forgiveness

This is a sobering passage, is it not? If the forgiveness of God is a massive ocean on which we are being invited to sail, it feels as though there may be dragons in the water! It is a frightening thing to consider how seriously God takes the matter of forgiveness both toward us and coming from us. But I want to begin by focusing on the awesome liberality of God's forgiveness.

It is interesting and appropriate that Jesus would use a financial illustration to make His point about forgiveness. In the parallel passage of this that is found in Luke 17:3-5, Jesus says this:

> **"Take heed to yourselves. If your brother sins against you, rebuke him; and if he repents, forgive him. And if he sins against you seven times in a day, and seven times in a day returns to you, saying, 'I repent,' you shall forgive him."**
> **And the apostles said to the Lord, "Increase our faith."**

Have you ever really considered the impact of the Lord's statement here? He is saying that if a person sins against you seven times in a day and repents, we are to forgive him. Put it in a real situational context. Your co-worker comes to you and says something critical and derogatory that is totally inappropriate and out of line. In a few minutes, she feels remorse, and she comes and asks forgiveness. But then she does it again. And again, she repents, seeking forgiveness. But then she does it again, and again, and again, and again, and again, asking forgiveness each time. And this is just one day! Then, to take it even further, in the Matthew 18 story, Jesus ups the standard from seven times to seventy times seven! Unlimited forgiveness.

How many of you sense you need a bigger heart? I am going to need more capacity to release this kind of mercy. We need faith! We need a profound depth of experience of the Father's love and forgiveness in our own hearts that will allow us to release mercy at this level. You see, this is why I believe the topic of forgiveness does not seem very potent to us. I believe that few of us have really come to grips with the fact that we desperately need to be forgiven, that God has indeed forgiven us, and that we are declared completely free from guilt. Further, I suspect that few of us have really had the power encounter that forgiveness is intended to be – the experiential reality of having the burden of sin lifted from our necks.

Instead of deeply encountering the God of fearsome forgiveness, we assume that He's sort of winked at our sin and has said, "There, there, it's okay. I know you couldn't help it." We have backed off from a biblical posture of dealing with sin because we want to be sensitive to hurting people. We don't want to turn them off to the Gospel, and so we emasculate the Gospel and make it powerless. Now the biggest thing that confronts us is that we must somehow forgive ourselves. Beloved, there is no biblical doctrine of forgiving yourself. It is a heretical idea born in the impotent pop-culture counseling mode that has been substituted for pastoral care in our churches, and it is powerless to deal with

the problem of guilt and shame. We do not need to forgive ourselves. We need to have a power encounter with the mercy of
God. We must come face to face with the awesome reality that
the holy and righteous God, in whom there is no shadow of
darkness, is a God of forgiveness. We need to receive His forgiveness in a way that brings us to our knees before the power of
One, who could condemn us, who has every right to condemn
us, but who has decided to forgive at His own great cost.

The Book of Numbers is not normally a book that really turns
my crank with spiritual insight. Recently, however, I was reading
Chapter 19 and was deeply impacted by a truth hidden in the
prophetic symbolism of the sacrificial system. Numbers 19 speaks
of the duties of the priests and includes the idea that for the sacrifice of purification, the priest was to bring an unblemished animal to be slaughtered and then burned as the offering for sin.
The perfection of the animal speaks of the perfection and beauty
of Jesus Christ. The priest was to take the animal outside the
camp – which speaks of Jesus, under condemnation, being
removed outside the city gates of Jerusalem – and slaughter it
there. Then he was to take the blood of that perfect sacrifice and
sprinkle it seven times on the altar. Seven is the number of perfection in the Scripture, so we are seeing the picture of perfect
forgiveness. Perfect, unlimited forgiveness from a God who does
not mark iniquities, because if He did who could stand? My
goodness! It is incredible.

In Luke's version of this parable, Jesus says, *"If your brother
sins against you, rebuke him."* The Greek word for "rebuke" is
*epitimao* and it means "to tax upon." It means to assign a mone-
tary value to the sin that has caused that person to be in your
debt, and then literally the word picture is, to "lay it on them."
And so when we hold someone in unforgiveness, we have taken
the debt of their sin against us and laid it on them and said, "You
shall carry this until you pay me back."

But the word "forgive," *aphiemi*, means literally that you take
that thing off from them and send it away. This is what the Father
pictured as He calls us into His realm of forgiveness – He takes

that debt from us and sends it away. We have the wonderful picture of Isaiah 53:6, that says, *"All of us like sheep have gone astray, each one of us has turned to his own way, but the Lord has laid up on Him the iniquity of us all."* The Lord had taken the bill and laid it upon His shoulders. He carried it to the cross and it was sent away! Therefore, it is in the contemplation of the cross of Christ that we will come to grips with the extent of what it cost God to have mercy on us. We will gaze upon Him whom we pierced, our hearts will be smitten with godly sorrow for sin, and the wonder of forgiveness will fill us with the fear of the Lord.

So in our story in Matthew 18 there are several points about the awesome liberality of God's forgiveness. First of all, the Master summoned his servant to settle his account. Some of the versions that you have say that this was a "servant," some say "slave." The word is *doulos,* and it means a bond-servant. It was a relationship that began in a slave/master arrangement, but as intimacy and friendship emerged between the slave and the Master, the slave could eventually be taken on as a son.

But this servant is summoned to give account because he owes the master 10,000 talents. The first thing I want to point out to you is there is a day of accounting. The Master does not say, "Well, we'll let bygones be bygones and just forget about this little thing." You see, sin matters! Sin is an offense against the very holiness and nature of God, and it matters in an ultimate way! That is why the price to pay for sin was so dear. The Scripture says that we are not bought with perishable things like gold and silver but with imperishable things – the precious blood of Jesus Christ. Sin matters! Therefore, there is a day of accounting.

I am glad about that. I am glad that the mercy of God does not leave me in my mess and just sort of pat me on the head as though it didn't matter. The mercy of God is a holy, glad thing that lifts me up and says, "You shall be My son, and you shall look like Me, you shall be holy, for I am holy." That is good news. He does not leave us in our mess. There is a day of reckoning.

For those that have had their hearts converted through trusting Christ, it is a joyful day of receiving our reward and coming into the eternal presence of our Lover and Bridegroom, Jesus Christ. But for those who have refused forgiveness, it is a day of terror and condemnation. It is a time when people will be faced with the tremendous cost that God paid to offer forgiveness, and those who have spurned His perfect offer will experience His perfect wrath.

Happily, today is still the day of salvation. We can still take advantage of Jesus' offer to forgive. And if you have never come to the Lord, if you have never brought the bill of sin to Him and fallen down before Him saying, "I cannot carry this any longer. I cannot pay this," the Lord stands with open arms today, in THIS day of salvation and says, "Come to Me, I long to pay the bill for you! I long to send it away from you that you might take your place as My child and My Bride."

## A Huge Debt

The debt that this servant owed was an immense thing. I did a little arithmetic on this debt – it was 10,000 talents of gold. A talent does not mean anything to us in our understanding, but in the cultural standards of measurement, a talent was 96 pounds of gold.[1] For ease of calculation, I will round it off to 100 pounds. As I write this in the summer of 2003, the price of gold is $344 per ounce. Ten thousand talents of gold at $344 per ounce comes to about $5.5 billion dollars. This guy owed his Master $5.5 billion. Ouch!!

You know, there are only a few guys in the earth that have that much money anyway. And this guy owed it to his King! Now what does that tell you about the King and His resources? I mean this King is rich! He has one guy that owes Him more than only a few people in the world have today, in this time of inflation. Ten thousand talents of gold – $5.5 billion dollars!

The second thing we notice in Matthew 18 is that the servant

---

[1] *International Standard Bible Encyclopedia*

had a completely unrealistic appraisal of his ability to pay back
the King. *"Be patient with me and I will pay you back everything."* I love the sense of humor with which Jesus reports the
Kings reply in verse 25: *"Since he did not have the means to pay
it back. . . ."* Really! It's this little dry humor that comes sneaking
out of Jesus, and I love that it's there.

Do you ever find that when you experience the mercy of God,
something goes off inside you and you want to make a vow? You
want to make promises to God and say, "If you will do this, I will
do better!" What we must understand is that until we have a
deep and powerful encounter with the fearsome forgiveness of
God, we will never do better. We don't have what it takes to do
better without the mercy and grace of God.

Having said that, the Scripture does give us the right kind of
vow to make to the Lord. In Psalm 50, the Spirit of God tells us to
bring a thank offering to the Lord and to call upon His name. The
Lord informs the people that He does not need their sacrifices.
He doesn't need them to pay the debt. It's a debt they cannot pay
anyway, so He says, "Here is what I want. Tell me 'thank You'
and ask Me for help again." That's it! Tell Him 'thank You' and
ask Him for more. God is massively kind and generous, and it
pleases Him to give good things to His children. The payback He
desires is our gratitude and our trust. That is the vow that is
pleasing to the Lord.

But this servant thought he could manage the debt, so he
tried to file an extension. "Be patient and I will pay it all back."
But this is an unpayable debt. You know, I did the arithmetic. A
slave's wage was one denarius a day. The dynamic equivalent in
our day might be someone that works for a union wage of $25
per hour, or $200 per day. At that rate, do you know how long it
would take to pay off $5.5 Billion? 27.5 million working days.
That's 75,343 years, with no weekends or holidays. How many of
you know that this guy is looking for a second job? You know, he
is looking for overtime! "Can I work the weekend?!" "Anybody
need a shift taken?" This guy has lots of work to do to pay this
thing back. That is why with that debtor's mentality, he goes out

and tries to extract a much smaller debt from his friend. He is in debt and needs the money!

But the debt of sin being what it is, his plea is touching in its sincerity, but it is ridiculous in its assumptions. He cannot pay this thing back. We do not now, nor will we ever have the resources to pay God back for our debt of sin, and without forgiveness, we are hopeless. Our only hope is in a God who is wealthy beyond comprehension, who is merciful, and who is generous.

The third point in this story is exactly that: the King that we serve is wealthy beyond comprehension and merciful and generous. We have the God that we need. The God we serve is the God we need, and He is ready to move in our behalf. I love Psalms 62:11-12, that says:

> **God has spoken once and twice I have heard this,**
> **that power belongs to God.**
> **And also to You, Oh Lord, belongs mercy;**
> **for You render to each one according to his work.**

Power and mercy belong to God. He has the ability and the willingness to do what we need.

Have you ever been in a situation where you have had the willingness to do something but you did not have the ability? Or, you had the ability and did not have willingness? That is probably even worse. But we serve a God that has the ability and the willingness to be what we need Him to be. Oh, that is good! He loves us, and with Him is power and mercy. He is wealthy beyond comprehension; He is wealthy enough to forgive that kind of debt. He is merciful. He is moved with compassion. The Greek term for "compassion" is *splagchnon,* which is picturesquely translated in the King James Version as "bowels of mercy." It talks about a gutsy forgiveness, that when God feels that compassion moving within Him, His insides turn over, and He is filled with the desire and the willingness to help those who call upon Him with a grateful heart.

When the Master hears the servant make his ridiculous promise to pay back the debt, His insides turn with compassion, and He does not respond to the servant's request. Rather, He answers him with the Father's heart. He forgives the debt, releases him, and lets him go. He did not forgive the debt and fire him, saying, "I do not want this guy working for me." He released him and let him go back to his ministry, his life, back to his service. In effect, he was saying to this guy, go out and live in the exhilarating freedom of fearsome forgiveness.

Why do I keep calling it "fearsome forgiveness"? If God is so willing and has the resources to do it, why must we come from that encounter with the fear of the Lord burning in our hearts?

It is because the Father absorbs the cost of the sin and pays it from His own resources. This cost is the blood of Jesus, which is priceless. When I was preaching this series at Metro Christian Fellowship, one of the sisters in the Fellowship told me a wonderful story, and I tell it to you with her permission. She came up during the ministry time after one of the messages to receive the good news of the forgiveness of God. Thirty years earlier, she had a child out of wedlock, was sent away by her family to have the child and give it up for adoption. When she came home after that experience, she was met by her father, who was the cranky accountant that many of us picture God to be. He gave her a little black book in which he had detailed all of the expenses of her pregnancy and her experience. He took her into her room, set that little black book on her dresser, and said, "There, now you remember."

How many of us know that little black books like that are about more than money? They are about things like shame, rejection, fear, and brokenness. Then every week, as she would bring home her paycheck from her job, she would hand her paycheck to her father. He would receive it, and then he would go into her room, take that little black book, and mark out a line of debt – week after week, line upon line, until the debt was paid. Perhaps you can relate to the burden of that weight of shame and guilt clouding every encounter with your father, the one who could forgive, but chooses not to. The world is filled with people living under just such a cloud of unforgiveness. They never know the joy of being set free from the debt, never believing that God would be the Father of forgiveness.

So, that particular Sunday during the ministry time, she was at the altar when the Lord opened the eyes of her spirit. She saw herself standing again in her bedroom and looking at that little black book on the dresser, when suddenly the door opened and Jesus walked in. He walked straight to that little black book, opened it, and stamped it "Paid-in-Full." Then He took that little book of her debt and flung it away! He sent it away. He threw it out! And He took a little white book that was a book of promise and hope, gave it to her, and said, "This is it, this is the Book of Salvation." He replaced the debt with hope. The debt is paid and cast away. His blood is enough. You owe God nothing, except to say thank you and ask Him again.

There is something in us that wants to try to pay God back. But what can we add to the blood of Jesus? Isaiah tells us that our righteous works are like filthy rags in comparison with the blood of Jesus. It is a very graphic term and I will not go into it, but Isaiah is saying that our effort at paying for righteousness is not helpful. What we do is not helpful.

## Indebted Slavery Instead of Sonship

Besides that, He does not want us to relate to Him in a slave mentality. That was the dilemma of the older son in Luke 15. But God wants sons that are partners with Him in mercy! Sons that have a party in their hearts! Sons that are rich in mercy and for-giveness, who know how to celebrate! The thing that the Father anticipates then in the aftermath of His mercy is that He will have a liberated servant who rejoices in forgiveness; a servant who is overwhelmed with joy in the knowledge that the debt has been taken away.

Do you remember the movie *The Mission?* It came out some years ago, and if you have not seen it, I would urge you to do so.

It is a story of forgiveness and mercy in the passion of the Kingdom of God. It involves the story of a mercenary soldier in South America many years ago. He was hired by the government to bring the Indian population into slavery, so he hunted them down. But then he became friends with a Jesuit priest who led him to Christ, and this mercenary slave trader became a missionary. He became one who would go up to the Indian villages above the great waterfalls to bring the Good News of salvation to the very people that he had hunted.

However, this redeemed slave-master still had the mentality of indebtedness, not of freedom in sonship. He was so overwhelmed with the guilt of his past life that he put all of his weapons of warfare in a big bag on his back and climbed up the falls. It became obvious that he could not carry the load; he could not do it. He stumbled, fell back, stumbled again, fell back again, and finally in the climactic moment of that scene, one of the Indians whom he had mercilessly hunted came over to him with a sharp knife. The tension of the moment is profound because you know that the just thing would be to put the mercenary to death. But this Indian man who had been led to Christ takes that knife and reaches behind the soldier, cuts his burden off, and casts it away down the waterfall. Then he takes his former enemy's hand and helps him up the rest of the way. Forgiveness! The burden is sent away! The soldier falls in a heap of thanksgiving and rejoices before his Father, trembling with the right kind of fear. How can this be! With You, O God, there is forgiveness; therefore, men fear You.

What the Father wants when He ministers forgiveness to us is that we get His heart for ourselves and our brothers and sisters. He desires that we become radical purveyors of mercy; not the unsanctified, meaningless kind of "mercy" that leaves people in their junk but the ferocious forgiveness of the Lion of Judah. It's the strong love that sets us on our feet and makes us sons and daughters, kings and queens. Strong mercy allows us to become the Bride of Christ that walks in power and authority alongside our King!

The servant did not get it. Instead of moving into his identity and destiny as a partner with the King, he chose slavery over sonship. It was a tragic thing. Verse 28 tells us

**That servant went out and found one of his fellow servants who owed him 100 denarii; and he laid his hands on him, and took him by the throat, saying, 'Pay me what you owe!'**

Instead of receiving forgiveness and walking in it, he retained a debtor's mentality. Therefore, he could not afford to forgive his fellow servant. You see, when we retain the debtor's mentality, then we have to extract things from people, because we owe. If he still had that $5.5 billion dollar debt in his mind, then it was important for him to get that 100 days wages to pay back the Master. Do you see how that connects?

Unforgiveness is a debtor's mentality. When we hold onto the things that God wants us to forgive in other people, it is because we still have not grasped the mercy of God in our own lives. We have not entered into thanksgiving, nor into joyfulness, nor into asking for more. A denarius, which was a days wage, was about the equivalent of $200. Therefore, 100 denarii would equal $20,000. Now on a horizontal plane, $20,000 is a substantial amount. If somebody owed me $20,000, I would make a note of it. I keep track of books, you know, that people borrow from my house. $20,000? I would pay attention to that! And yet when it comes into comparison with what this guy owed the King, it is so small as to be ridiculous.

Let us take it down to manageable numbers because hardly anyone can relate to $5.5 billion dollars. So, I just knocked off some zeroes and picked an arbitrary number that is easy to work with–$55,000. I did a little bit of arithmetic just to see percentages. Let's say the guy owed the King $55,000. Some people make that in a year, you can kind of relate to $55,000. Do you know what the comparable debt of this other servant to this guy was? If he owed the King $55,000, the other guy owed him ten cents. Ten cents, total! In comparison to his debt, his friend owed

him ten cents. If you collect ten cents every 100 days, do you
know how long it takes to collect $55,000? 27.5 million days.

And so, he goes to his friend, and he extracts his ten cents
and goes, "Psheww, I've only got 27,499,900 days left. I am gonna
be okay!" That is the ludicrous reality of unforgiveness.
Unforgiveness is ludicrous. It puts us in torment, it does not help
us pay the debt because the debt is unpayable, and it just makes
us not think right. But God has invited us into a new kind of
economy. Since the payment Jesus made was sufficient, we are
forgiven, and get this now, we have no debt. Say this out loud: "I
do not owe God anything." Really! I do not owe God anything.
Meditate on that for about a billion years. There is no debt,
except to say thank you and to ask Him for more.

God desires that we become His partners in mercy. Because
there is no debt, there is no need to extract from others. He wants
us to stand alongside with Him and pour out forgiveness on all
who will come. He invites us to absorb the cost of their debt,
knowing that His resources are more than enough to cover it. He
says, "Here, I will pay it for you, come and forgive them. Give
them forgiveness; take their debt into yourself. Take it upon
yourself and then bring it to me."

So we come to Him loaded with the painful things of human
relationships. How many of us know that it is in the closest relationships that the seven times a day comes into play? Seven times
a day, again and again the incessant little stuff of intimacy faces
us with the choice of forgiving. If we don't make that choice in
the right way, we end up in torment, imprisoned in our own attitudes of bitterness. The only safe place is abandonment to the
mercy of God.

## A Lesson in Resource Management

When my son Dave was 12, we decided to exercise a little
introduction into financial management. I told him, "Son I am
going to increase your allowance and here is what you are
responsible to manage: your clothing purchases, your sports

equipment, your recreational stuff, your book purchases for school, your piano lessons; in short, the stuff of your young life. You know you need to manage the money and here are the things you are responsible for." As I was detailing the things for which he was responsible, this sort of anguished look came over his face and his eyes filled with tears. I said, "Son, what's going on?" And he said, "Well, I cannot afford all of that stuff!" My heart broke for him as I realized he had missed a very important part of the conversation. I said, "Oh son, I am going to give you the money!"

You see, the thing that was overwhelming him was that he was still thinking on a $5.00-per-week economy. He did not understand that when he entered into partnership with me in the management of his life, the resources were mine to give him. He would have all that he needed. It was a question of managing the resources, not of generating the resources. Do you see this? It is a question of management. If we have an old economy, a debtor's mentality, we do not have nearly enough resources to forgive. But if we will partner with the Father, we have an expense account that is limitless.

Here is your expense account. Paul says in Ephesians 1, "I pray

**that the God of our Lord Jesus Christ, the Father of Glory, may give to you the spirit of wisdom and revelation in the knowledge of Him, the eyes of your understanding being enlightened that you may know what is the hope of His calling, what are the riches of the Glory of His inheritance in the saints, and what is the exceeding greatness of His power toward us who believe according to the working of His mighty power which He worked in Christ when He raised Him from the dead and seated Him at His right hand in the heavenly places, far above all principalities, and power and might and dominion in everything name that is named. Not only in this age, but in the age to come."**

There is your bank account! Take it and forgive everything

that moves! Look for ways to spend mercy and come back to the Father and say, "Oh, this is great! Thank You, thank You, give me more!" And we go out and do it again. And you know what happens? Revival! The Father's house gets full, the lost get captured by the beauty of Jesus, and heaven breaks loose on the earth.

## The Torment of Unforgiveness

Those who refuse to live in the power and grace of the Father's liberal forgiveness end up in torment. In the torment of unforgiveness, in the debtor's mentality, we forget that what people owe us is nothing compared to what we owe the Father. When this man went out, grabbed that other servant, and began to choke him, the other servants came to the Master and said, "This is not right." They reported his unfaithfulness in placing another servant back under bondage, back under a debtor's mentality, and the King was then forced to respond to that first servant according to his choices. You see, it was a matter of choice for that servant, not a matter of ability. The text says that when the first servant's friend asked him to be patient, he was not willing to be generous but demanded his money back. Having received such mercy that he should have been trembling with holy fear, he was not willing!

When it comes to forgiving one another, it is not a matter of ability; it is only a matter of choice. For we have the resources of the mercy of God. It is like floating in that vast ocean of the mercy of God, and someone comes and asks us for a cup of water and we say, "I don't think there is going to be enough for myself." It is ludicrous to hang on to it. The King's mercy had been granted for the asking. The King's expectation was that that same heart of forgiveness would be expressed by the servant. When it was not, by the servant's own choice, he was returned back to debtor's status and became accountable for his debt once again. And he was turned over to the tormentors.

I believe that the "tormentors" mentioned in this story are in reality demonic pressures that are released upon the mind and

soul of an individual who refuses to live in the grace of forgiveness. Fear and guilt plague their thoughts. The anger of unresolved relational issues haunts them. They find themselves having conversations with themselves in their cars, cursing others
and vindicating themselves, and there is no rest. They are miser-
able people and are driven to all sorts of devices to try to calm
their fears.

Do you know the torment of unforgiveness in your own life?
Do you know the anguish of driving down the street in the car by
yourself, and, all of a sudden, the list of people that owe you
comes to your mind? You find yourself getting smaller in your
heart. The grace and mercy of God dissipates out the window,
and you become like Scrooge, spewing "Bah, humbug!" to all who
hear. I tell you, you do not have to live there anymore. We are
invited to a new economy. We are invited to be converted in heart
into the economy of the King. But when we refuse to forgive, we
place ourselves in a prison of torment that is plagued with shame
and fear. We will stay there either until we pay the debt that is
impossible to pay or until we embrace the heart of the King and
become like Him, His partners in reconciliation.

### Partners in Reconciliation

I believe that this servant's only way out of torment was to
appeal to the King again, to receive His mercy again, and to
begin to extend mercy in the way the King intended it. If he
would have just come and asked to speak with the King one
more time, saying, "Oh, Lord, I see what I have done, have mercy
on me again!" And guess what, it would have been compassion
that took over again, and He would have gone, "Oh son, that is
what I wanted all along!" The King would have released him
again into the reality of his partnership. Until he was willing to
do that, he would spend his life tormented by his own failure
and the failure of others.

The forgiveness of God is an awesome thing. His mercy and
His grace empower us to become free and to be agents of recon-

ciliation on His behalf. The Psalmist is right: "There is forgiveness with you, Oh, Lord, and therefore, You are to be feared." God is inviting us forward to come out of the torment of unforgiveness and to step into the glorious freedom of the Kingdom of God. He demands that we become free. He loves us too much to allow us to stay in our smallness and in our slavery. He is so insistent upon our freedom that if His goodness does not motivate us, He will allow us to be turned over to torment until we surrender to His mercy. What choice will you make today? Will you cower in your little prison of self-preserving unforgiveness? Or will you rid yourself of it and dive in and entrust yourself to the mercies of God?

In his book *Future Grace*, John Piper has written a wonderful paragraph which is worth the purchase price:

> **The dark valley breath of bitterness cannot survive the high paths of faith in future grace. Grudges demand the valley vapors of self-pity and fear and emptiness. They cannot survive the contentment and confidence and fullness of joy that come from satisfaction in the forgiving God of future grace.**

Today God is inviting you to freedom. He is inviting you to come and receive His forgiveness. He is inviting you to tell Him "Thank You" and to ask His forgiveness for the burden of sin. He wants to release you from the smallness and ingratitude of your heart. He is beckoning you to come in and expand your soul in His dwelling place. This is His pathway to liberty in your life, and there is no other.

CHAPTER

# THE NURTURING FATHER

## 6

JOHN 6:25-58

I love a good story. I love to tell stories and to hear a story well-told. There is a delight and joy in telling a good story that is unique for both the storyteller and those who listen. The skilled telling of a good story captures the imagination and communicates truth in wonderful ways. We were created with an innate sense of appreciation for good stories, and every culture throughout history has understood their power and influence. Stories, legends, and myths give meaning and definition to those who hear. We identify with the characters in a compelling drama, finding hope for our places of despair when the hero wins the battle. We find relief for our feelings of fear and helplessness when justice comes for the underdogs as they are rescued from the bad guys at the last moment.

Jesus was a master storyteller who fully understood that the history of God's people is the best story, the most romantic, tension-filled, and gloriously resolved drama of them all. Jesus knew that the hearts of His beloved people would be captured by the tales of their own past. He could skillfully weave a tale in such a way that the listeners would become characters in the true drama of life. He knew they would recognize themselves in the stories, and if their hearts were ready, they would respond in ways that would transform their very existence.

It was a common thing for Jesus to pick up on the daily situations that He encountered as He walked with His followers and turn those situations into storytelling sessions. His methodology was to take the events of life and discern the human issues that were involved in those events. He would then bring instruction that would draw the hearers closer to His heart. Just such a thing is recorded for us in the Gospel of John Chapter 6, where Jesus is instructing His disciples using one of the most well-known stories in all of their history. It is the story of when God sent manna from heaven to nourish the people of God during the journey from Egypt to the Promised Land. I would encourage you to take a few minutes and read John 6:25-58 so that you will have a fuller understanding of what follows.

The context of this story is that on the previous day, Jesus had miraculously fed the multitudes on the side of a hill near the Sea of Galilee. Then, during the night, He had told His disciples to cross the Sea and had come walking to them on the water in the midst of a great storm! What a night that must have been! Then, on the day of our story, the crowds were wondering where Jesus had gone and finally found Him teaching in the synagogue in Capernaum on the other side of the lake. They knew He had not gotten into the boat with the disciples, so they were surprised and understandably confused.

As they asked Jesus how He got there, the Holy Spirit revealed their hearts to Him. He saw that they were interested in Him not because their hearts had been captured by the truth that He was revealing, but because He had fed them in a situation of hunger. This would be a good guy to have around – one who could take a kid's lunch and turn it into enough food for 5,000 men plus their families! Think of the implications for a community that was accustomed to living in poverty! So Jesus sized up the situation, and He saw an opportunity for a story that would reveal the heart of His Father in a unique and powerful way.

**Focusing on the Wrong Food**

Jesus points out to His listeners the futility of focusing their labors on acquiring food that is not eternal. He calls them to give themselves to the pursuit of real food, food that will put them in touch with eternal realities and not merely satisfy their bodily appetites. In doing so, Jesus is once again dialing up for them their own history. He invokes their awareness of such passages as Isaiah 55, where the prophet urged the people to come and buy food and drink that had no earthly cost but led to eternal satisfaction of heart and soul. He is using indirect language to remind them of Psalm 42 and Psalm 63, where the longing for the spiritual water of God's presence is the familiar theme. But the real bait that Jesus is putting out for His audience is their most famous story – that of the Exodus from Egypt and the provision of manna from heaven that the Father released through the prayers of Moses. Jesus wants to teach them about true and living bread, true nurture, and the fact that He Himself will give them the true bread for which they are searching. So He throws the baited statement out there to see if they will go after it:

> **Do not labor for the food which perishes, but for the food which endures to everlasting life, which the Son of Man will give you, because God the Father has set His seal on Him. (John 6:27)**

And indeed, they do take the bait. Their immediate response is to ask Jesus' opinion of what they should do to release the power and provision of God's Kingdom in their lives. Jesus answers them with a call to believe in Him as the one whom God has sent. This statement sets the hook in the jaws of the questioners, and their next question fully sets the stage for the teaching Jesus is ready to bring:

> **Therefore they said to Him, "What sign will You perform then, that we may see it and believe You? What work will You do? Our fathers ate the manna in the desert; as it is written, 'He gave them bread from heaven to eat.' " (John 6:30-31)**

The real issue is now on the table. The Jews want to see a miraculous sign that will validate for them who Jesus is. The standard of measurement for such signs is the giving of manna from heaven during the time of the Exodus. Their hero was Moses, whose leadership was validated in their eyes because when he prayed, manna was given. Their mistake was that they had set their focus on the person of Moses, making him a hero of mythical proportions instead of seeing that the manna was given by God in a divine prophetic preview. God was providing for their immediate needs in a marvelous way, with heavenly food that seemed plain, but in fact, it carried all that they needed in terms of nourishment. But He was also giving them a prophetic sign that one day He would send them His own Son as the Bread of Life. He would be the true food that would be the source of their life forever. Though He would seem plain, like just a man, He would in fact be the Son of Man and Son of God. Jesus is the Living Bread and Living Water that would nourish and sustain them for all eternity.

Jesus answers their question with classic brevity and power:

**Then Jesus said to them, "Most assuredly, I say to you, Moses did not give you the bread from heaven, but My Father gives you the true bread from heaven. For the bread of God is He who comes down from heaven and gives life to the world."**

Jesus is doing a massive thing in this little paragraph. He is declaring a truth that is enormously powerful in its implications yet speaking subtly enough so that if the eyes of their understanding are closed, they will miss it. With the "Most assuredly, I say to you . . ." phrase, Jesus is once again establishing His authority to speak ultimate truth. Whatever the Jews had thought to be right understanding was now being redefined by one who had authority to redefine it. Then, He simply states the fact that He Himself is the fulfillment of the prophetic picture of manna and is the true Bread of God, sent down from heaven to give life.

The Jews respond with minimal perception, and the tension mounts:

**Then they said to Him, "Lord, give us this bread always."**

**And Jesus said to them, "I am the bread of life. He who comes to Me shall never hunger, and he who believes in Me shall never thirst. But I said to you that you have seen Me and yet do not believe. All that the Father gives Me will come to Me, and the one who comes to Me I will by no means cast out. For I have come down from heaven, not to do My own will, but the will of Him who sent Me. This is the will of the Father who sent Me, that of all He has given Me I should lose nothing, but should raise it up at the last day. And this is the will of Him who sent Me, that everyone who sees the Son and believes in Him may have everlasting life; and I will raise him up at the last day."**

**The Jews then complained about Him, because He said, "I am the bread which came down from heaven." And they said, "Is not this Jesus, the son of Joseph, whose father and mother we know? How is it then that He says, 'I have come down from heaven'?" (John 6:34-42)**

The Jews stumbled at what Jesus was saying. They claimed to understand, but their understanding was limited to a superficial perception of Jesus' identity as a man. So He responds to them one more time:

Jesus therefore answered and said to them,

**"Do not murmur among yourselves. No one can come to Me unless the Father who sent Me draws him; and I will raise him up at the last day. It is written in the prophets, 'And they shall all be taught by God.' Therefore everyone who has heard and learned from the Father comes to Me. Not that anyone has seen the Father, except He who is from God; He has seen the Father. Most assuredly, I say to you, he who believes in Me has everlasting life. I am the bread of life. Your fathers ate the manna in the wilderness,**

and are dead. This is the bread which comes down from
heaven, that one may eat of it and not die. I am the living
bread which came down from heaven. If anyone eats of this
bread, he will live forever; and the bread that I shall give is
My flesh, which I shall give for the life of the world."
(John 6:43-51)

## The Need for Real Food

The dynamic that Jesus is addressing here assumes that God
has created people with the need for nourishment that comes
from outside themselves. We are not self-sustaining; we do not
regenerate on our own. Rather we require substance and nurture
from outside ourselves in order to maintain life. There is no perpetual motion machine; we don't have what it takes to live in an
ongoing way by ourselves. We cannot feed ourselves; we must
receive nurture that is from outside of us.

The way God has created us is that life would come in relationship with Him. He created us to walk in intimacy with Him,
to draw life from the fellowship with Him that comes in various
ways. When Adam and Eve used to walk with God in the garden
in the cool of the day, they were doing more than just examining
flowers to see if Adam was doing a good job gardening. They
were being nurtured together, drawing their life from the life and
the presence of God. All life was in Him, and from Him, through
Him, and unto Him, and it was in the context of intimacy and
relationship with the Father that Adam and Eve would thrive
and find their strength.

God had provided food for the couple, but in reality, their
strength came from His blessing and presence. He had given
them work to do, but it was not slave labor. It was the joyous,
playful co-management of the creation walked out in the context
of intimate and ongoing friendship with God. He had given them
authority over the things He had made, but it was not so they
would find their significance in how powerful they were. Rather,
God intended them to embrace Him, and in this embrace, they
would realize their true dignity and destiny – heirs of God and

partners with His eternal Son.

It was no accident that the enemy came cloaked in deceptive beauty to draw the couple's attention to another form of nurture. Satan began to focus their eyes on material nurture, tempting them to see the vehicle of nurture as the source itself. Satan's approach was to cause Adam and Eve to question what God really said, and his purpose was to bring doubt into their minds about the truth of God's attitudes toward them. They began to question whether God really had their best interests at heart. They wondered whether He would really satisfy their desires for significance, intimacy, and destiny. Satan appealed to their true sense of greatness, but he convinced them that they would need to grasp it themselves, instead of trusting the Father to give it to them by grace in the right time.

In contrast to this, consider the words of David as he voices his confidence in the perfect timing of God' provision:

**The eyes of all look expectantly to You,**
**And You give them their food in due season.**
**You open Your hand**
**And satisfy the desire of every living thing.**
**(Psalms 145:15-16)**

You see, the Father's plan is to give us all things in the right season. There is a perfect timing that the Father has set in His own heart for the release of all things. He will release everything that will be for our blessing, our maximum pleasure, and glory. God is absolutely focused on maximum glory for Himself, and His strategy for this ultimate glory is the thorough beautification of His sons and daughters. He will present us to His Son, our Bridegroom Jesus, perfectly prepared, radiant, and dazzling as His Son's suitable counterpart, His crowning glory.

There is a wonderful picture of this presented to us in the second chapter of the Book of Esther. The King's eunuch, a man named Hegai, has received Esther as one of the candidates to be the King's new Queen. In the aftermath of the fall from grace of the former queen, Vashti, a search has been instigated to find a suitable partner for the King who will share His glory and authority. Esther, the picture of the Bride of Christ in this story, gains the favor of Hegai. This man represents the Spirit of the Father as he prepares her for the King's pleasure. He provides her with twice the normal allotment of preparatory materials, gives her seven handmaidens to help beautify her, and oversees the process of her cleansing and training so that she will capture the King's heart in a maximum way.

This is how the Father deals with us. For the sake of His own pleasure, to present us faultless and radiant to His own Son, He gives us everything we need, just at the right time. But the strategy of the enemy, as it was with Adam and Eve, is to try to convince us that God is not trustworthy in this process. Satan wants us to believe that if we are going to have a destiny and an identity, we have to seize it for ourselves. We have to take control of our own development and clutch at the sources of nurture. We must seize the things of preparation, so that we can beautify ourselves. It is a tragic mistake to believe the enemy's lies.

## The Assertive Pursuit of Nurture

None of this is to say that we are to be passive in the pursuit of nurture for our souls. The craving for nurture is perhaps the most powerful urge that we have as human beings. People who find themselves in a deprived situation will do nearly anything to find food, to survive, even if it means making choices that seem subhuman.

Using a much more positive image, I remember when my older daughter, Alyson, was a baby, and how she loved to nurse at her mother's breast. I mean, this little girl loved to eat, and when it was time to eat, there was nothing that could stand in the way! She would scream until we got the message, and then at the first hint of Mary's response, she would begin to burrow through clothing, totally committed to latching on to the source of her nourishment. She didn't care who else was in the room, or where

we were, or if it was convenient. She wanted nourishment, and
she wanted it now!

I believe that none of us has grown out of that craving for
nurture. There is a craving in every person for that sense of fulfillment of body, soul, and spirit, and we will do whatever it
takes to satisfy that hunger. The strategy of the enemy throughout history has been to play on that passion. He tries to get us to
mistrust the true Source of this nurture and to grasp for things
that were never intended to supply what we need. The things of
life were intended at best to be vehicles of sustenance, means by
which the Father's nurture would come to us. They were never
intended to be the source of that nourishment. Because of the
enemy's influence and our foolish choices, it has been man's consistent pattern to ignore the true Source of nurture and chase
after bread that does not satisfy.

All through history, God's people have heard His voice in the
distance saying, "Come to Me, come to Me! I am your life, I am
your substance, I am your provider, I am your healer, your sustenance, come to Me." But the record of mankind is the record of
people turning away from that voice and going to things that seem
more tangible. We want things we can touch and feel and grasp.
We have turned away from the nurturing Father. The history of
God's people is filled with those kinds of tragic stories, from the
nation of Israel to the modern Church, including you and me.

Why do we make those kinds of choices so consistently, when
all of history shouts to us of the futility of that approach? Do you
remember from Chapter Three where I spoke of the propensity of
sheep to go their own way? We can become determined to point
our noses in a direction that God has not given us, and do our
own thing. We may even have heard His voice calling us in
another direction, but we listen to the siren song of the evil one.
Then we decide that we know better how to attain the things that
will give us life and success. We think that if we can just get into
that relationship, or that job situation, or buy those clothes, or get
connected with any one of a thousand things, our life will be better and be more fulfilled. We ignore the Father's voice that draws

us to the place of intimacy because we think it's wasted time. We long for fulfillment, and we think, "If it is to be, it is up to me!" How tragic and foolish!

Listen to the wisdom of the writer of Proverbs as he describes the voice of folly that calls us to the wrong kind of nurture:

> **A foolish woman is clamorous;**
> **She is simple, and knows nothing.**
> **For she sits at the door of her house,**
> **On a seat by the highest places of the city,**
> **To call to those who pass by,**
> **Who go straight on their way:**
> **"Whoever is simple, let him turn in here";**
> **And as for him who lacks understanding, she says to him,**
> **"Stolen water is sweet,**
> **And bread eaten in secret is pleasant."**
> **But he does not know that the dead are there,**
> **That her guests are in the depths of hell.**
> **(Proverbs 9:13-18)**

Our society is full of that sort of thing. The pathways of history are strewn with the catastrophic results of people looking for nurture in the wrong places, from the wrong sources. We foolishly heed the voice of the evil one who calls us away from the truth of God's provision to things that seem more accessible. We join ourselves to work thinking that we will find provision there. We join ourselves to the right health club thinking that we will find relationship there. We join ourselves to the right church thinking we will find significance in the system. We join ourselves to illicit relationships thinking that we will find fascination there.

The strategy of the enemy has been to keep up the façade that there is life to be had at those sources. He wants you to think that if you will buy bread from this store it will give you nurture, if you buy drink from this place it will give you nurture. And the woman folly cries out loud, *"Come and eat and drink here, stolen water is great, food eaten in secret is great."* Did you notice what the end of that proverb is? *"Little did they know that the dead*

*are there, that her guests are in the depths of the grave."* When
we join ourselves to those sources thinking that we will receive
life and significance there, we actually take into ourselves the
brokenness of the people and the systems from which we are
drinking. Instead of receiving the life of God, we open ourselves
to the fractured and polluted reality of ungodly systems and people, and we begin to die. The dis-integrated state of our society
and culture is a direct result of people's determined efforts to
find life and meaning where there is none.

I'm continually amazed at the persistent use of sensual
images in our culture to promote and sell virtually everything
that is marketed. We do not sell products; we sell sex appeal, or
the promise of happiness, the illusion of success and influence.
The ads proffer the false nurture of sensual fulfillment, and we
fall for it again and again. Thousands of times a day, we are all
bombarded by the voice of the foolish woman – "come in here,
and buy, and drink from this well." It is the wellspring of death.

Why do we think that the enemy's number one strategy is the
breakup of the family, the shattering of intimate relationship
between husband and wife? It is because God designed things so
that in the home the child would learn to drink nurture from the
healthy mother and eat the bread of identity and encouragement
that the healthy father offers. God's plan was for the child to
drink the water of substance there. By feeding the spirit in that
kind of setting, the child could grow into maturity, understanding how to look to the Heavenly Father as the source of all good
things. But many homes are populated by adult children with
broken souls and unresolved identity crises, people looking for
meaning in external settings. Their own spirits are fractured, and
satisfaction cannot be found in their pursuit of the American
dream. They have nothing to offer one another, let alone the children that are sired between them. The world and the Church
today are full of malnourished, weak, and abandoned people,
without hope, filled with heartache and loneliness. They are fractured and estranged with no understanding of how to eat and
drink the life that is in God alone.

The people of God ache; we have the hunger pains of little children who have not had enough to eat and it aches and aches. So we run from one place to another, from one dry well to another, from one broken person to another, from one job promise to another, from one house to another, from one city to another, on and on, *ad infinitum, ad nauseam.* We run back and forth, back and forth again and again looking for nurture, and we can't find it. The Rolling Stones were prophets in their time when they screamed that they could "get no satisfaction."

## The Reality of True Nurture

Now, that is the bad news. But the good news is that our Father God has something to say to us. He has spoken to us in His Son Jesus Christ, who says to us, "I am the Bread of Life, I am the Living Water." Jesus did not come in anger to hungering and thirsting people, pointing a finger and saying, "You get your act together, you straighten up!" He was in touch with the desire that was latent within them. Jesus knew what it was for us to crave the Father's nurture because He made us like that. It was His idea for us to live in such intimate relationship with the Father that life would continually flow to us, even as it continually flowed to Him from before the beginning of time. He walked in such intimacy with the Father that He could say to His disciples, "I have food that you know nothing about! My very food is to do the will of my Father, and He constantly feeds me with lovingkindness, revealing His will and purpose to me, day by day."

The Father-heart of God is the heart that beats with a passion to meet the craving of your heart for nurture. He comes to you today and He says, "I am the Fountain of life, and I have made My life available to you through My Son, Jesus. Come and drink from Me through Him, and you will never be thirsty or hungry again!" The Father's heart is so open to us, and His life is so available.

I once took a ministry team to El Paso, Texas, to visit the ministry of Father Rick Thomas, a Catholic priest who served the poor in El Paso and the in the neighboring city of Juarez, Mexico. While there, we had opportunity to minister in the prisons and mental institutions of Juarez, and the Lord showed us powerful things. In the jails of Juarez at that time, the policy was that there was no food for the prisoners. Unless family members would bring food, or someone else would have mercy on them, the prisoners simply would go without nourishment. Father Rick and his team would come and share the message of the Gospel with these men and women, calling them to a relationship with Christ, and then they would feed the prisoners. The inmates would come out of their cells into a courtyard where they were given a very nourishing drink, loaded with vitamins and other good stuff, and a rich whole wheat bread that would sustain them. One could not obtain this kind of bread at the local market – it was strong bread! I tell you, it was a revelation to see these men and women receive this bread as life itself! They were hungry, and it was the Father's good pleasure to feed them. In the same way, Jesus calls us to see that He is the Living Bread, the one from whom we might draw all our life.

### Three Ways to Receive True Nurture

How do we take this heavenly nurture into ourselves? What is the process of filling ourselves with Him so that our lives shine forth with the glory of the Lord revealed in our faces? I believe there are three simple realities involved in living in the fullness of the nourishment of God's presence. I want to mention the first two now and save the third until the end of the chapter. The first is to turn away from false sources of nurture, and the second is to live in the presence of Jesus.

As I write, I have just completed a week of ministry in Kona, Hawaii, at the University of the Nations. This is the well-known school associated with Youth With A Mission, or YWAM. It was my privilege to have several of our staff members from the International House of Prayer in Kansas City with me to share in the week. Seth Parks, a marvelous young worship leader from

IHOP-KC, had led worship one evening, and the presence of the Lord had been sweet, right from the beginning. After the meeting, a young man in the congregation approached Seth to ask him how it was that there was no "warm-up," that the moment the music began, the presence of the Lord was felt.

I can tell you why. It is because Seth lives in the presence of Jesus. The Son of God has become Seth's food and drink. He has turned away other sources that would pollute the stream of his life, and his one fountain is the Son of God. Seth and his young bride Erin have made the Most High their dwelling place; they have turned off the world of entertainment in order to worship Jesus. They have embraced a lifestyle of fasting and prayer because they want to live on His presence and be nurtured by His life. They have decided that their identity is not in what the world thinks or in the level of income they can produce. They have decided that Jesus will be enough for them, and He is proving Himself to them day after day. Therefore, when Seth strums his guitar with the first stroke of a worship set, he is merely inviting others into the place where he lives full-time. The table is set all the time, and the Bread of Life is released, and the Water of Life flows freely.

The first step toward living in the fullness of the Father's nurture is to realize that it is only found in His presence. Therefore, turn away from the other stuff, and turn toward Him. Develop a life of prayer and fasting. Refuse the delusion that meaning and fulfillment can be found in your own pursuits. Doing it your way isn't going to get it done. Oh, Beloved, how I wish I could communicate to you the passion in my heart as I write this! The Father longs to take you in His arms, to release to you His provision of life and love, but He will not force you to it. He will only invite you to leave the false nurture of horizontal pursuits and come to Him in the place of worship.

You see, it is in the place of worship that we drink from His life. It is as we minister to Him in Spirit and in truth that the sweet wine of His presence is released to us. The Bread of Life is broken for us as we encounter the Word of God, the Man Christ

Jesus, revealed in the Scriptures. There is no secret path, no exotic thing that we have to do to find this life. It's right in front of us, every day and in every setting. We simply turn away from the illusionary things that promise fulfillment but never deliver, and turn toward the beautiful Man Jesus as He reveals the Father's love to us day by day. We do it in the place of personal and corporate worship. It happens in the place of meditating on the Scripture, chewing on it, and speaking and singing to oneself the truths of the Word of God. As we give ourselves to worship and to His Word, we find our souls being fed with the real food, the real drink of His life made available for us. It is so easy and simple, but there is no other way.

A picture comes to my mind as I write, and it is the image of a newborn kangaroo finding its place of nourishment. The joey is born, and then it has to fight its way through the mother's fur into the pouch where it latches on to the source of its life, drinking the mother's milk. The young kangaroo is determined and assertive in getting to that place, for its very survival depends on it. Then once it is attached, it stays there until it reaches a place of maturity and strength.

I want to urge you to worship like that, to seek the secret place of the Most High with that kind of determination. Understand that your very survival depends on finding this true place of nurture, and understand that the Father has made it readily available to you. Push through the maze of empty distractions, and find the place where His life flows. He is eager to be found, eager to provide all that you need. As you pursue His presence in worship, as you seek out His reality in the Word of God, your soul will be strengthened. You will begin to live in a vibrant and healthy reality that is the very presence of God.

I believe that for many of us, especially those from a conservative Protestant tradition, this involves the re-awakening of an understanding of the communion celebration. For too long we evangelicals have missed out on the beauty and power of the Lord's Table because we have reduced it to a mere memorial, instead of seeing it as the power encounter it is intended to be.

Jesus declared in John 6:55-56 that there is a reality and power in the ingestion of the bread and the wine that takes us deep into intimacy with Him:

**For My flesh is food indeed, and My blood is drink indeed. He who eats My flesh and drinks My blood abides in Me, and I in him.**

This statement invokes more than a mere memory. This is power encounter language, and I want to urge us to reconsider our ways, to delve deeply into the mystery of His Presence in the bread and the wine. I believe that the Holy Spirit would be pleased to restore to us the sense of awe and wonder that pervaded the early Church when they celebrated the Lord's Table. He will help us to understand and experience again all that Jesus has for us in fellowship with Himself.

The final dimension of drawing nurture from the Heavenly Father is to become involved in a vibrant community of growing believers who are experiencing together the life of worship and growth in the Word that I have just described. I have listed this one last because it only is effective in the light of the first two realities. One of the main reasons that church relationships are disappointing to people is that we think we can find life in the fellowship without giving ourselves to worship, the ingestion of the Word, and to prayer. The "first thing" of loving God with all of our heart, soul, mind, and strength must always be the first thing, or the "second thing" of relational connectedness will never be effective. But once the first thing is in place, the presence of a vibrant community life with other believers is essential.

God loves to reveal Himself to us through one another. In the place of mutual ministry, the Father draws us into the same kind of partnership with Himself that Jesus knew. We share together in the life of ministry that was His own food and drink. The Father desires that we would be channels of His life to one another. He wants us to embrace one another in holiness and godly affection, to care for one another, and to serve one another in the

Spirit of Christ. In that way, our lives get broken in the right way. We get poured out in loving self-sacrifice even as His life was broken and poured out. We drink from Him through one another, and the life of the Body of Christ is strengthened and built up.

This happens in families that are emerging into healthy relationships and in small groups that are giving themselves to loving one another. It comes as we pray together, as we labor side by side, as we serve one another in the Spirit of Christ. It comes as we learn how to embrace one another in holy ways again, having our brokenness healed in the love of Jesus. It needs to happen in families, between married couples and between parents and their children. It needs to happen in small groups and in ministry times, encouraging one another with the words of Jesus as we see each other after the Spirit of God.

As this happens, there are going to be some results that begin to emerge. The passage in John 6 asserts that there will be satisfaction for the thirsty, a certain place of refuge that will never end. Proverbs 9 tells us that as we drink from the life of the Father, there will be wisdom and understanding that will come forth in our lives. But there is one passage that really grabs my heart on this matter, and it is found in the Book of Isaiah. I simply want to paraphrase verses 15 and following of Chapter 60. It says that although you have been forsaken and hated with no one traveling through (no one interested in your existence), although you have been turned out alone by yourself, although you have been forsaken and abandoned like a starving child by the side of the road thrown in a dumpster someplace, God will make you the ever lasting pride and the joy of the generations. You will drink the milk of nations, you will nurse at royal breasts, and you will receive the nurture of the Father. The result is that you will know that the Lord is your Savior, your Redeemer, the mighty one of Jacob. He will take the inferior stuff of your life and bring the superior, He will take that which is faulty and bring that which is pure to you as you nurture from Him, as you drink from Him. He says,

**I will make peace your governor and righteousness your**

**ruler. No longer will violence be heard in your land, but you
will call your walls salvation and your gates praise. The
sun will no more be your light by day nor will the bright-
ness of the moon shine on you, for the Lord will be your
everlasting light and your God will be your glory. Your sun
will never set again and your moon will wane no more; the
Lord will be your everlasting light and your days of sorrow
will end. Then will all your people be righteous.**

When? When you have drunk from royal breasts, when you
have nurtured from the Father. Then you will possess the land
forever, the fullness of the Kingdom of God.

I urge you with everything that is in me: drink from the
Fountain of Life, the Heavenly Father revealed in the person of
Jesus Christ. He is all you need.

## CHAPTER 7
# THE FATHER OF HUMILITY
### LUKE 14:1-14

O ne of the great joys that is growing in my own experience is the practice of contemplating the nature of God revealed through the life of Jesus as recorded in the Gospels. When Jesus walked the earth, His fundamental objective was to demonstrate the true identity of the Father in the crucible of actual human existence. Revealing the Father's true identity and nature was the passion of Jesus' heart, and it is interesting to observe how the disciples struggled to embrace the God that Jesus was revealing day by day. The expectations of their hearts were so different from actual truth that time and again Jesus had to remind them that He and the Father were one entity, and that the Father was just like Him.

At the very end of His time on earth, Jesus makes this statement, recorded in the seventh verse of John 14:

**"If you had known Me, you would have known My Father also; and from now on you know Him and have seen Him."**

Philip responded to Jesus with the request that the Lord would disclose the Father to them, and that if He did so, it would be sufficient to meet the longings of their hearts. Philip's appeal reflects the basic cry of the human heart to know the Father and to have His person revealed to us. But Philip had missed the fact that Jesus' entire time with them had been for that very purpose, so Jesus responded to him with a gentle but focused admonition:

**"Have I been with you so long, and yet you have not known Me? He who has seen Me has seen the Father."**

"He who has seen Me has seen the Father." What a massive statement that is! It means that as we consider the encounters of Jesus in the Gospels, meditating upon the ways in which He dealt with weak human beings day after day, we come to the clearest exposition of the nature of God, this Father that we long to know.

In Luke 14:1-14 we have another window into the character of the Father as revealed in the life and teaching of Jesus. It is a passage that reveals the humility of God, the fact that He is the Father of humility. Jesus is once again in a situation that has tension written all over it. He has clearly established His authority as a Rabbi, a respected teacher of religious truth. The clarity of His teachings plus the miraculous power that accompanied Him wherever He went has made Him the focus of much attention from every group in the culture of the day.

Because of this increasing notoriety, Jesus becomes the particular focus of the Pharisees' suspicious eyes. They want to study Him, to watch Him, and try to figure out a way to control Him. His words and works are undeniably powerful. Many people are being affected by them, so He has to be taken seriously. Therefore, He is invited to be the guest of honor at a dinner party hosted by one of the Pharisees. Now in the normal experience of the world system, such an invitation might be seen as a real opportunity to climb the ladder of influence. After all, the power people have taken notice! However, Jesus has steadfastly refused to play the normal game that religious leaders all over the earth have played for millennia. It is the game focused on gaining position, power, and authority within the human structures of society. It just seemed that Jesus didn't care at all about that, and that He wasn't shy about confronting the system that promoted such attitudes.

## A Wrong Understanding

One of the viewpoints that Jesus confronted with regularity was the Pharisaical misunderstanding of the Sabbath day. Intended in God's heart as a day of withdrawal from normal activity into a place of encounter with God, it had become just another religious requirement. The Sabbath was attended by harsh, judgmental perspectives, and mostly devoid of the tender intimacy and refreshment for which it had been established.

So when Jesus observed a man suffering from edema attending the dinner, the tender mercies of His heart clashed with the religious expectations of the Pharisees. Jesus focused the question of whether it was lawful to heal on the Sabbath. On the day of rest, was it legitimate to bring rest to a person weary in body and soul because of a difficult and most likely fatal condition? The Pharisees had no answer for the question. One can only imagine the frustration and emerging rage that must have been in their hearts as the shallow and merciless façade of their religious understanding was exposed for all to see.

When Jesus healed this man, He was demonstrating one of the most amazing realities of the character of the Father, and that is that God is the Father of humility. He is the God who takes the low place, preferring to serve the needs of the hurting person instead of focusing on His own short-term benefit. Jesus embraces the place of servanthood for the purpose of blessing and releasing broken people into wholeness, and it is His glory to do so. Jesus was living out His intimate partnership with the Father before their eyes. He had articulated His principle of operation in another Sabbath-day encounter, the situation of the man at the Pool of Bethesda in John 5, where He said these words:

> **"My Father has been working until now, and I have been working. Most assuredly, I say to you, the Son can do nothing of Himself, but what He sees the Father do; for whatever He does, the Son also does in like manner. For the Father loves the Son, and shows Him all things that He Himself does." (John 5:17, 19-20)**

Jesus lived in a perpetual Sabbath, a place of rest in the Father's delightful love and mercy that expressed itself through the constant revelation of what the Father was saying and doing. The Pharisees were upset because Jesus was "working" on the Sabbath, but they completely missed the point. The central purpose of the Sabbath was to bring weary people into an encounter with God the Father that would give them rest. Jesus was not arrogantly flouting the Law; He was standing in a place of humility, tenderly fulfilling the purpose of the Law. He wanted to lead wounded and weary people into encounters with the living God. His service to the sick and broken was a demonstration of humility that came straight from the Father's heart.

**The Struggle for Honor**

The situation intensifies in the subsequent verses of Luke 14. Jesus observes one of the most common symptoms of brokenness in human beings – the struggle to be in a place of recognition and honor. There was a definite order of place, a protocol for the seating arrangements at such banquets, and the guests were clamoring for the highest available seats. They wanted others to see them there and know their relative importance in the social hierarchy. Unfortunately, some of them had claimed seats that were previously assigned to someone else, and they were now enduring the humiliation of being re-seated in a lower place before the watching eyes of the dinner guests.

This situation points out an inherent tension that exists in all our hearts. In the mind and spirit of every human being there lives a sense that we ought to be somebody and that others ought to notice us and make room for us. I believe that this sense is a God-given thing, a deposit of identity that is part of the nature of God in whose image we are made. He is the King of kings and the Lord of lords! He is the matchless Creator, the All-Wise and Omnipotent God before whom every knee shall surely bow, and we are His sons and daughters! We were created to be kings and queens, joint-heirs with Christ of the mysteries of God. We were designed to rule, destined for greatness, and the awareness of that design is part of what motivates us day by day.

Because of this, I believe Jesus was very tender in His corrective remarks to the guests. There were other situations in which His own disciples had grasped after greatness, and Jesus never rebuked them for that desire. In fact, I believe that Jesus was affirming of their desire for greatness. But He always brought focus to that desire, instructing them that their greatness was not in external position or authority. Rather, Jesus taught that greatness was rooted in the knowledge of the Father, in the place of intimacy with Him.

In Luke 10, Jesus sent the disciples out to minister in the power of the Holy Spirit. They returned with great gladness, telling the stories of how the power of God had been manifest in their situations! They were ecstatic that the authority of Jesus had been released to them and that the demons of hell had fled at their rebuke in the power of His Name. And Jesus celebrated with them! The text says that Jesus rejoiced with them in the Holy Spirit, but then He drew them to the place of reality, the place of relationship with the Father. He instructed them not to focus their joy in the fact of spiritual power and authority, but to rejoice mainly in the fact that their names were written in heaven. In other words, that the Father knew who they were. That's the place of greatness! The Father knows your name! Rejoice in that, and all other things come into focus.

## Attaining True Greatness

The difficulty comes in our perception of how greatness is to be attained. In our brokenness, we have lost the sense of pleasure and delight that God has in His children, the Fatherly delight that was the root-system of Jesus' life. Because we have sinned, we have fallen from grace; we have lost the understanding that God's full intention is to glorify us as His children. In our fallen condition, we have assumed that we are responsible for our own exaltation, and so we aggressively strive for power. We assert ourselves, grasping for the highest place because in our hearts we rightly sense that it belongs to us! At the same time, we are filled with the fear that we will not be given our due, not recognized for the great people we are. The problem is that we do not know the Father's heart of humility that will exalt us fully as we give our lives to Him and learn to live in the character of Jesus.

So, Jesus begins to instruct the banquet guests on how to attain maximum pleasure and glory, and His methodology is stunning! He articulates a principle of heavenly glory that is a direct reflection of the nature of God. Jesus is living out this principle in their midst, and we will examine that in a moment. The principle is stated in verses 10 and 11:

> **"But when you are invited, go and sit down in the lowest place, so that when he who invited you comes he may say to you, 'Friend, go up higher.' Then you will have glory in the presence of those who sit at the table with you. For whoever exalts himself will be humbled, and he who humbles himself will be exalted."**

Do you see the heart of the Father here? His chief concern is to release maximum glory in the experience of His children, but He says you have to go about it in the right way. Humility must become the foundation stone of exaltation! It's how the Kingdom of God works, and there is no way around it because it's founded on the very nature of God as a humble Father. If we understand that Jesus' teachings about humility are designed to produce maximum glory in our experience, then we will begin to conform our desires to heavenly reality. Then we will begin to experience the fruit of exaltation in our lives.

Most of us have not had much experience in a spiritual culture in which God is seen to be for us. We're not accustomed to a perception that the Father is delighted with His children while they are in the process of coming to maturity. Most believers, if they have a sense of God's pleasure at all, assume that His pleasure can only be realized after we become mature. We assume He'll be happy only after all the issues of our lives have been addressed and we are fully conformed to the image of Jesus. We can hardly imagine a God who would delight in us while we are still growing, while we are still weak and inconsistent, stumbling heavenward. We see ourselves in our struggle with pride, and we hate the fact that we wrestle with it. We are conscious that it was at the level of pride that Satan captured the first humans and snared them with delusions of grandeur so that they forfeited the life in God they were intended to have.

What we fail to understand is that what Satan appealed to in Adam and Eve was not a *delusion* of grandeur. It was the very real awareness that greatness was their destiny. Their sin was not that they desired greatness, but that they became convinced that God did not have their greatness as His focus. They believed the lie that if they were to be great, they would have to seize greatness for themselves. Satan convinced them that God could not be trusted to release greatness to them. So instead of entrusting themselves to the Father in humility, waiting for Him to exalt them in due time, they grasped after greatness on their own terms. Instead of waiting for Him to release greatness by the power of His grace, they assumed the responsibility of achieving greatness by their striving.

This choice on their part has had disastrous consequences through all human history. Perhaps the results of proud behavior have never been more eloquently articulated than in the fourth chapter of James' open letter to the Church of the first century:

> **Where do wars and fights come from among you? Do they not come from your desires for pleasure that war in your members? You lust and do not have. You murder and covet and cannot obtain. You fight and war. Yet you do not have because you do not ask. You ask and do not receive, because you ask amiss, that you may spend it on your pleasures.**
>
> **Adulterers and adulteresses! Do you not know that friend-**

**ship with the world is enmity with God? Whoever therefore
wants to be an friend of the world makes himself an enemy
of God. Or do you think that the Scripture says in vain,
"The Spirit who dwells in us yearns jealously"?
(James 4:1-5)**

The root of all human conflict is the unresolved issue of
pride, the soulish striving after a glorious destiny that we know
should be ours. But instead of receiving it from the gracious hand
of our Father, we turn to our own devices to grasp by aggressive
striving that which He would give us freely. We wrongly believe
that God is against us and not for us, that He is a God who with-
holds, not a God who gives. We are mistakenly convinced that if
we give ourselves to Him, He will squelch us. We think that we'll
spend eternity as lobotomized caricatures, bored and pathetic,
floating around heaven carrying harps we don't know how to
play.

How far from the truth this is! God is Himself the greatest
Being in the universe, and it is His desire that we be fully conformed to the image of His Son. In the Man Christ Jesus, all the
fullness of the Godhead dwells in bodily form. Since you are His
Beloved, it is His desire to make you great. But we must understand that the pathway to greatness is humility and servanthood.
It's the path that Jesus took, and it is our path as well. He calls us
to humility, not in order to suppress and render us impotent, but
precisely because it is the way He expresses greatness.

## Humility is Rooted in the Character of God

I want to focus on several passages that are representative of
the humility that is characteristic of the Father's nature. First of
all, in Genesis 1 we have the record that the first interaction
between the Father and His newly created humans was to "bless
them."[1] The Hebrew word used here is *barak*, which means to
kneel before someone either to bless him or to receive a blessing.

---

[1] See *Genesis 1:28*

In this passage, the Creator kneels before Adam and Eve and serves them everything they will need for enjoyment and fulfillment. He presents them with the delight of procreation, with the destiny of dominion, and with the enjoyment of provision, thereby releasing to them amazing dignity and significance.

Further, in Genesis 2:19, God brings to Adam every beast of the field and every bird of the air "to see what he would call them"! This is a significant picture of humility on the part of God. He gives that kind of dignity and authority to people for the purpose of sharing with them in the rulership of the created order. The reality that the uncreated God would stoop to a relationship of partnering with created beings, to dignify them, to lift them up to His level, is simply staggering. One gets the impression that this God is not threatened concerning His place of authority. Rather, He uses that authority to strengthen and release His people in order that they might share in His glory.

Perhaps the greatest example of God's humility in the Genesis accounts is the fact that He presents Adam and Eve with the choice to relate to Him or not. God establishes a scenario in which created human beings have the freedom to choose to have relationship with Him or to reject Him to pursue their own agenda. It is such a stunning concept – God placing Himself in a posture of waiting to be chosen by human beings! And not only that, but the kind of posture He chooses is the posture of a Father and a Bridegroom! His heart is filled with longing and desire, and He opens Himself to being rejected for the sake of lesser gods. This is incomprehensible! It is beyond understanding that God would subject Himself to this kind of vulnerability, waiting to be chosen by created beings in a way that actually affects His heart. The more I contemplate the wonder of this, the more my heart is staggered at the thought. The God of the universe has humility at the center of His being!

In the life of King David, God paints a prophetic picture of the character of His own Son, Jesus, and that life is characterized by great humility. David consistently places his confidence in the character of the Father. David trusts God to establish the promises over David's life in His own time, without manipulating those promises or trying to seize control of their fulfillment. He focuses on serving and obeying, leaving his position and safety in the hands of God. He stands in the declaration of God's grace in his life. He pays no attention to the taunts of men as he approaches the battle with Goliath, choosing to believe in God's faithfulness rather than the apparent reality of the situation. He submits to an unrighteous king even as Jesus submitted to human authority, commending his life into the hands of the God who has the real authority to establish kings or to uproot them. David lived in that place of unrelenting confidence in the kindness of God, believing the promises of destiny that God had spoken to him. He simply waited upon the Lord, and thereby became the prophetic picture of Jesus the Messiah.

Another prophetic picture of Jesus that is compelling in the revelation of His humility is found in Isaiah 42. One of the great Servant Songs of the Book of Isaiah, verses one through four give us a persuasive portrayal of the style of the Son of God. He has the identity of the Servant, upheld by the strong hand of God. This reality alone should cause us to embrace servanthood as a lifestyle! The servant is upheld by the hand of God! I want to live in that place, don't you?

The Spirit of God rests upon this Servant, and His task is to establish justice, to set things right to the ends of the earth. His style is neither abrasive nor self-centered. He is not publicity hungry, and His priority is the gentle treatment of the broken and weak. He is resolute and determined and will not be denied in His pursuit of justice. This is a God of humility, and the coast-lands wait with eager anticipation for His Law to be established. Even the creation has sense enough to crave the leadership of this kind of Servant!

Consider such prophetic Scriptures as these that speak of God's delight in those that have a heart of humility. First, there is a declaration from the Psalmist:

**Though the LORD is on high,**
**Yet He regards the lowly;**

**But the proud He knows from afar.**
**(Psalms 138:6)**

The Lord, from on high, regards the lowly. This implies a focused and particular consideration for them, as opposed to the distance He keeps from those who are proud.

Then, we have insight from Isaiah:

**For thus says the High and Lofty one**
**Who inhabits eternity, whose name is Holy:**
**"I dwell in the high and holy place,**
**With him who has a contrite and humble spirit,**
**To revive the spirit of the humble,**
**And to revive the heart of the contrite ones."**
**(Isaiah 57:15)**

The clear sense of the Isaiah passage is that this Holy One considers the contrite and humble human spirit to be an appropriate dwelling place for Him, as suitable as the high and holy place of heaven! The High and Lofty One is at home in the heart of contrition and humility!

There is yet another picture of God's humility from Zechariah:

**"Rejoice greatly, O daughter of Zion!**
**Shout, O daughter of Jerusalem!**
**Behold, your King is coming to you;**
**He is just and having salvation,**
**Lowly and riding on a donkey,**
**A colt, the foal of a donkey."**
**(Zechariah 9:9)**

This prophetic promise, fulfilled in the life of Jesus in Matthew 21:4-5, straightforwardly declares that the King of justice and salvation has a lowly nature. He is in His very character a King of humility. It is no act, no feigned posture taken for the sake of the media with the goal of impressing the voters. This King is really humble! It's His nature, and because of that, He enjoys being with those of like heart and mind. He prefers the company of humble people. So, when He finds them, He tests them to demonstrate the genuine nature of their humility, and then exalts them to His own presence to share in His rule.

## Jesus' Humble Approach

With this description of the character of Christ established in the Old Testament, we can see His gentle and low-key approach to life and ministry for what it is. He is a God of humility coming in lowliness to bring salvation to the peoples of the earth. So as we read the Gospel stories and see Jesus coming to earth as a baby born in a cattle stall to a poor couple, we begin to see that God really intends to live out this identity of humility. We see Him coming as a Servant, not in obvious glory, but in the style of a gentle man who serves the needs of people day in and day out. He is led only by the voice of His Father as revealed to Him by the Holy Spirit. We see God with skin on, being available, accessible, and touchable. He is not removed from us; He is one of us. He is not protected by a cadre of bodyguards with the assignment of keeping the crowds away from Him. Whenever the disciples try to take that posture, He admonishes them and instructs them to allow the people to come to Him.

Every time He touched a sick person and healed them, He was bringing justice to the earth, one person at a time. Every time He spoke into a person and revealed their true identity to them, He set things right in the present situation, bringing the Kingdom of God to the earth. He took His signals from the Father alone, standing in the humble reality of what the Father said about Him. He was not influenced by the opinions of men. He submitted to unthinkable things – the Son of God being baptized in a dirty river, in order that He might carry us in His heart to the place of fulfilled righteousness. He went willingly to the wilderness, driven there by the Holy Spirit, in order to be tested by the Devil himself. Imagine that! God being tested by Satan! It is unthinkable that God would put His own Son in such a position, but that is the nature of a humble God. Carrying us along with

Himself to the place of testing, the Son of Man withstood the wiles of the evil one and time after time chose the way of the Father instead of the way of ease. In doing that, He established once and for all that there was a Man who, under the extreme pressure of the enemy's tests, would obey the Father. There would be one who would not seek His own way but would live under the humble motto of "Not My will, but Yours be done." This consistent behavior established His identity as the Second Adam, and it gave to Him the right to bring forth a whole new race of humble, obedient sons and daughters.

In all of this, Jesus was the living fulfillment of the ancient hymn of the Church recorded in Philippians 2:5-11. Precisely because He was exactly like the Father, He made Himself nothing and took on the very nature of a servant. He laid aside the glory of heaven and wrapped Himself in garments of flesh so that He could live out His Father's own nature of servanthood. He called Himself the Living Water and not only because He was refreshing to all who come to Him. He took that name specifically because it is the nature of water to flow to the lowest place in order to fill that which is lowly. He continually humbled Himself, even to the point of death on a cross, which was the place of unspeakable horror and shame. He willingly became the accursed one so that He could redeem the most broken and ashamed among men. He did it so that no one could claim that God does not understand, that God doesn't know my pain. He took upon Himself the sin of the world and bore the shame that drove us from the Father's presence. He drank the full cup of the wrath of God, hanging naked and forsaken so that He might have eternal relationship with human beings like you and me. This God is stunning. He is unbelievable in His humility. He is the God we need, and He is the God we have.

### Humility and Exaltation

Therefore, God highly exalted Him. Because He poured out His soul unto death, was numbered with the transgressors, bore the sin of many, and made intercession for the transgressors, God has given Him the portion of the great. Because He perfectly lived out the Father's nature and held nothing back, the Father has given Him the Name above every name, that at the Name of Jesus every knee shall bow, whether in heaven or on the earth or under the earth. The government shall be upon His shoulders, and of the increase of His rule, there shall be no end. This is our King. He is the humble God.

It is no wonder then, in the light of who Jesus is and how He exemplified the nature of God as the Father of humility, that on the day of His exaltation He is honored as the only One found worthy. Recorded in Revelation 5, the angels and saints, the four living creatures and all the elders fall down before Him and declare that He is worthy to receive all power, all riches, all wisdom, all strength, all honor, all glory, and all blessing! Jesus Christ, the exact representation of the Father, is worthy to receive all these things because He left all the glory, became poor, and gave Himself for broken people like me. He is highly exalted because He humbled Himself even unto the death of the cross.

It is for these reasons that Jesus observes the striving and grasping sons in the parable of Luke 14, and in effect says to them, "O brothers, if you only understood how the Kingdom of God really works. It's about humility! You must understand that the Father's heart is lowly and gentle, and that He seeks for people of like mind and spirit so that He might dwell with them. Take the low place, not because that's all you're worth, but because when you live in His character, your exaltation at the hand of the Father is inevitable. You can trust Him to exalt you if you will understand His nature and act like you are one of His."

So in the light of these things, how do we live as sons and daughters of this Father? How do we walk through life as the Bride betrothed to this King? We do it first of all by becoming convinced that He is really like this. We study the Scriptures, meditating on the stories of Jesus, and the testimonies of those who knew Him well. We consider His long-suffering and patience with foolish people, and we reflect on His tenderness in dealing with us. We invite His Spirit to speak the truth to our hearts and declare the Father's true nature to us. From these meditations, we form our perception of His character and nature, agreeing with the biblical presentation of what God is like.

Secondly, we develop the practice of placing our lives into the hands of this humble God who loves to lift up those who are contrite in spirit and broken in heart. Little by little, we begin to trust that He really does have our best interests at heart, and that, therefore, we do not need to be primarily concerned about our own well-being. We begin to understand that the circumstances of life are designed to bring to the surface places in our hearts that are still captured in unbelief and mistrust. We embrace those circumstances as God's appointed helpers. They assist us in rooting out places of doubt and fear that keep us from living in exhilarated abandonment to His goodness and sovereignty. In the times of testing, we choose the truth that is revealed in the Word and in the testimony of Jesus, instead of believing our own soulish opinions about God and what He is up to.

Finally, we begin to live in relationship with other people as though these things are really true. We begin to prefer one another, confident that the Father sees us and loves it when we act like Him. We resolutely refuse anxiety about our own well-being, choosing instead to seek the well-being of others ahead of our own. We begin to have dinner parties for the poor, simply because God likes them, and because they can't begin to pay it back. We refuse to take control of our circumstances in order to ensure our own comfort. Rather, we commend ourselves into His hands, giving Him all the options. We spend ourselves on the poor and the broken, knowing that in doing so we are acting like He acted, demonstrating that we are indeed the suitable counterpart for this radiant Son.

Beloved, I tell you that this Father of humility is watching over you. He has incomprehensible honor and glory in store for you as you embrace the character of His precious Son. Do not fear to take the lower place, but entrust yourself to Him, and He will exalt you at the proper time. It's how life works.

## CHAPTER 8

# THE INVITING FATHER

## MATTHEW 22:1-14; LUKE 14:15-24

There is a particular truth of Scripture that moves my heart most in this season in my life. It is the reality that the ultimate goal in the heart of the Father for relationship with human beings is to prepare us for the Wedding Feast of the Lamb. There is going to be a wedding; the King of kings is the Bridegroom, and the Bride is His people adorned with righteousness, fully prepared by His own power to be His perfect counterpart.[1] It is this reality that provides the impetus for evangelism in a wonderful way, because it speaks to one of the fundamental longings of the human heart – to be loved eternally and exclusively by Someone who is dazzling and excellent.[2] The message of the Gospel was never intended to be "stop sinning or you'll go to hell." It was not even primarily to focus on the idea of receiving the forgiveness of Jesus and going to heaven when we die. Though both of those things are true issues that must be faced, they are not the central things that burn in the heart of God. Rather, they are the means to a startling and almost unbelievable end.

---

[1] For a full treatment on this topic, see my book *Bridal Intercession: Authority in Prayer Through Intimacy with Jesus*, Oasis House, 2001.
[2] See the great song of adoration recorded in *Song of Solomon 5:10-16*.

The primary message of the Gospel in the heart of Christ has always been this: "There's going to be a wedding! The King is in love, He's chosen His Bride, and it's you! So, come to the celebration!" Since this is the matter that burns brightest in the heart of the Father, it becomes the primary topic of Jesus' final teachings. Again and again through the last chapters of the Gospels, we find Jesus addressing the reality that the Kingdom of God is like a man preparing a wedding feast for his son. That is precisely the analogy used in the parallel texts of Matthew 22:1-14 and Luke 14:15-24. As I consider this presentation of the Father, I will use these two texts interchangeably so that there may be a harmonizing of the components of the story.

As we saw back in Chapter Four, Jesus was in attendance at a Sabbath meal. He had already used the occasion to introduce the topic of the wedding feast, teaching about humility in that context. He had pointed out in a gentle yet direct way that seeking high position was not the way of His Kingdom, but rather that His Father is a God who values humility of heart. I can only imagine how awkward and uncomfortable everyone must have felt as his own heart was exposed in front of everyone else.

As so often happens in that kind of situation, some poor soul felt the need to say something to try to break the tension. Feeling the strain of the moment, one of those sitting at the table with Jesus makes this comment: "Blessed is he who shall eat bread in the Kingdom of God." Now this is the kind of statement that in Jewish culture is called a *shibboleth*. A shibboleth is a type of cliché that is spoken to sound spiritual and wise when in reality one simply doesn't know what else to say. It's the equivalent of something like "what will be, will be" or "boys will be boys"; some vapid phrase that sounds good but is actually pointless. The guy making this comment is not really giving voice to a deep insight that is being gained through Jesus' teaching; rather, he is trying to extricate himself and the rest of the guests from the awkward feelings generated by Jesus' comments.

It doesn't work because what this man doesn't realize is that the Kingdom of God has in fact come into their midst. The King

Himself is sitting with them, and they are now eating at His
table. It was the day of their visitation, and they did not recognize it, and therefore their judgment would be great. Rather than
allowing the moment to slip away, Jesus seizes the opportunity
and presses the issue of His Father's agenda even further. If the
dinner guests thought they were uncomfortable up to this point,
they were in for a surprise. What Jesus was about to say would
be devastating to the religious leaders, while at the same time
being delightful to the peripheral folks who felt they had no
place at the table. Once again, Jesus the Rabbi is using the familiar principle of *remes*, where with just a few words he is drawing
forward a clear, historical context for what He is going to say. By
the time He has finished His first sentence, all His listeners know
that Jesus is speaking about the great Feast at the end of the age.
In the following paragraphs, I have outlined the components that
form the content of His unspoken understanding.

**Invited to a Feast**

The setting for this teaching from Jesus is a dinner party, a
small feast hosted by one of the Pharisees and attended by a certain number of invited guests. The comment made by the man
referring to the coming feast of the Kingdom gives us an insight
into the Jewish mindset behind the whole idea of feasting. The
Jews understood that there is a great Feast to come, an eschato-
logical celebration anticipated by all who are aware of it. This
concept is fundamental to Jewish thinking. All of the feasts pre-
scribed in the Old Testament were founded upon the revelation
of heavenly reality given to Moses, who wrote down the guidelines based on what he had been given by Yahweh Himself.

God had commanded the Israelites to have three annual
feasts[3] in which the whole community of Israel was to gather and
celebrate the bountiful grace of the Lord. They were to be joyful
events, and they were mandatory in nature. All of these feasts are

---

[3] See *Exodus 23:14-19*

powerful prophetic pictures of the salvation that we have through Jesus Christ, and I would urge you to give time to the study of these feasts in the Scripture.[4]

Then, in an incredible climax to the His instructions concerning the feasts, God actually invited Moses and Aaron, along with seventy-two of the Elders of Israel, to come up into His Presence and experience the heavenly Feast! Recorded in Exodus 24, it is a stunning account of God's mercy and generosity to the leaders of His people:

> **Then Moses went up, also Aaron, Nadab, and Abihu, and seventy of the elders of Israel, and they saw the God of Israel. And there was under His feet as it were a paved work of sapphire stone, and it was like the very heavens in its clarity. But on the nobles of the children of Israel He did not lay His hand. So they saw God, and they ate and drank. (Exodus 24:9-11)**

My heart pounds with wonder and holy envy at the very thought of being in the actual Presence of God, sitting at His table, and eating and drinking with Him. And they survived it! Unbelievable! I long for the day when I'll be at that table with Him!

This historical event was the root system of comprehending all the celebratory events called "feasts." The clear understanding of the Jewish community was that all such celebrations were in anticipation of the great Feast to come. So when the man at the table uttered his shibboleth, he was articulating the common understanding of the day.

### The Feast is a Wedding Feast

The Feasts of the Lord were types and shadows of what is to come, giving the Jews of the time a partial understanding of

---

[4] See also *The Feasts of Israel*, by Kevin J. Conner, Bible Temple Publishing, 1980.

God's purposes. But it is through the teachings of Jesus and the Book of Revelation that we are able to give a fuller interpretation of the idea of the Feast. It is not merely a dinner party; it is the great Wedding Feast of heaven, the Marriage Supper of the Lamb that is being pictured here in Luke 14. In Matthew's account of this parable, it is explicitly clear that the feast to which all were invited is in fact a wedding feast, given by the Master of the estate on behalf of his son:

> **And Jesus answered and spoke to them again by parables and said: "The kingdom of heaven is like a certain king who arranged a marriage for his son, and sent out his servants to call those who were invited to the wedding. . . . (Matthew 22:1-3)**

When this passage is understood alongside Revelation 19:5-9, a clear picture emerges that the anticipated Feast is indeed the celebration of the eternal joining of Jesus Christ with His beloved Bride:

> **Then a voice came from the throne, saying, "Praise our God, all you His servants and those who fear Him, both small and great!" And I heard, as it were, the voice of a great multitude, as the sound of many waters and as the sound of mighty thunderings, saying, "Alleluia! For the Lord God Omnipotent reigns! Let us be glad and rejoice and give Him glory, for the marriage of the Lamb has come, and His wife has made herself ready." And to her it was granted to be arrayed in fine linen, clean and bright, for the fine linen is the righteous acts of the saints. Then he said to me, "Write: 'Blessed are those who are called to the marriage supper of the Lamb!'" And he said to me, "These are the true sayings of God."**

Needless to say, there would be great eagerness in the heart of God for this Feast to take place, and the anticipation of the attendance of His beloved people – not merely as guests, but as the Bride! – would be equally great.

## It is the Wedding Feast of a King

Once again, Matthew's version of this parable helps us understand the importance of this particular celebration. It is not merely a feast; it is not even merely a wedding feast. It is the wedding feast of the King's Son, and therefore it is a feast of the greatest possible importance. The King's feasts are pictured in the Word of God as lavish and generous in their scope and provision.[5] How much more of His bounty would the King pour out on the wedding feast of the Heir to the Kingdom!

Given all of these factors, it is easy to understand that the King would expect the glad participation of the citizens of His Kingdom in the feast He had prepared. Our texts tell us that when everything was ready, the King sent out servants *"to call those who were invited to the wedding."* There is an underlying assumption in the passage that the initial invitations had gone out much earlier, informing the guests that the wedding was scheduled, and asking them to make plans to attend. The understanding was that they had all agreed to come when the time was right, and so now the servants were being sent out to beckon them to the event, in fulfillment of their commitment.[6] The King, as the host of the feast, would have made preparations based on the number of guests that had agreed to come. So you can imagine His dismay when all those that He had invited suddenly had excuses that prohibited them from attending the celebration. This would have been seen as a gross insult in any situation, but the fact that it was the King who was being disregarded takes the drama of the story to unimaginable levels.

## Three Flimsy Excuses

Again, the combination of the texts in Matthew and Luke gives us a full picture of the contempt for the King shown by those who

---

[5] See Esther 1:4, where the purpose of the King was to "show forth the riches of His glorious Kingdom."

[6] See the article on "Banquets" from *The New Unger's Bible Dictionary.*

refused to come to the celebration. We are told in the first place that the recipients of the summons *"made light of it, and went their ways."*[7] To "make light" of something is to regard it as insignificant, not worthy of attention. The recipients of the invitation exhibit their disdain for the King by being completely uninterested in the invitation. This is astonishing to me as I consider the story, for I'm beginning to have a sense of the beauty and majesty of this King. When He invites, it is wisdom to say "yes."

Luke tells us that there were three categories of refusal that summarized the responses of the people. First, there is the individual who says, *"I have bought a piece of ground, and I must go and see it. I ask you to have me excused."* Now at first hearing, this seems like a reasonable request; who would not want to see a piece of ground that had been purchased? No doubt, the land was expensive, and the individual wanted to see the land. But in reality, it is just an excuse. Who would buy expensive land without first looking at it? This was not a crucial examination of the land with a time frame for completing a deal hanging over his head. This was the excuse of a man who was too preoccupied with his own agenda to come to the celebration of the King! Even though he had made the commitment to come, when the actual summons was delivered, he opted out due to his careless attitude. What is being communicated here is a complete disdain for the King, for His pleasure, and His desire that His people should share in the day of His gladness.

The same holds true for the second invitee. The excuse that comes from this man is that he has bought five yoke of oxen, and he must go look at them. Again, this sounds at first like a legitimate thing until you begin to think about it. Five yoke of oxen is ten animals. No one is going to make a large investment that is central to your livelihood without first knowing the value and the excellence of what is being purchased. This man would have seen these animals before buying them. He would have tested them to see if they were good animals, able to work together to

---

[7] See *Matthew 22:5*

accomplish the tasks common to the agricultural life of the day. Besides, if a man was wealthy enough to purchase ten animals like that, he would probably send a servant to size up the animals or to bring them back to the home place. No, this isn't a real reason not to attend the banquet. He's just finding an excuse.

There is a third response which, at first hearing, seems to be the most legitimate of all the replies, but in fact turns out to be the least reasonable. The third man informs the servants that he has just gotten married and, therefore, is taken up with the duties of ministering to his new wife. That certainly seems appropriate, until you realize that newlyweds were given exemption from all responsibilities for the first year of their marriage. They had no obligation to be part of anything that didn't appeal to them. They would be exempt from military service, from civil responsibilities, and from social expectations. There was no pressure on them to come. However, what must be understood is that they were exempt from these things *precisely so they could spend their time in celebration!* There was no one who should have been more excited to come than this young couple, for they would have known more than anyone the joy of the wedding feast. They simply didn't want to come.

The situation turns much darker after these lame excuses have been given. Some of the respondents not only ignore the beckoning of the King, they in fact become violent, attacking and killing the servants who were sent out to deliver the summons. The unthinkable happens! The citizens of the Kingdom, having given their promise to come, have fully ignored the King in the fullness of time, even resorting to violence to resist His invitation.

### Reasons for the Responses

The responses of the people to the King's request seem unbelievable to us, especially in the light of the beauty and generosity that is so evident in the life of Jesus and in His portrayal of His Father's character. So the question that comes to me is "why?" Why were these people so disdainful of the King's invitation?

Why were they so uninterested that they made up lame excuses, even resorting to violence to put off the will of the King? A couple of things come to mind.

In the first place, I am reminded of the banquet of another great King, recorded in the first chapter of the Book of Esther. Clearly a prophetic picture of the relationship between King Jesus and His Bride, the Church, this book presents the King as a kind and gracious monarch, most generous to all who come to His celebration. Yet in His generosity, He is forbearing and allows His guests to participate at whatever level they choose. There comes a cataclysmic moment in the celebration when the King bids His Queen, Vashti, to draw near so that the visiting nobles may enjoy her beauty and honor Him who is her Beloved. In response to His summons, the Queen sends her regrets, saying that she cannot come because she is preoccupied with her own celebration. In her refusal, she dishonors the King, the very one by whose grace she has the resources to celebrate in the first place! His full intention is to bring her into a celebration that is far beyond what she can produce on her own. He desires to celebrate with her in the intimacy of their marriage! She can have more than she can imagine and have the King's heart as well! Therefore, her retort is unthinkable!

This response results in Vashti's disgraced dismissal as Queen, and the resulting initiative to find a girl who is worthy of the King's affections. That girl turns out to be Esther, whom I imagine as a poor shepherd's daughter taken from the countryside who becomes the King's Beloved in one of the great romantic stories of history.

Do you see the parallels here? The Father, pictured here by Jesus as the gracious King, has summoned to the celebration the people who are in fact betrothed to be His Son's Bride! These were the people of the covenant, and from the Father's perspective, the covenant was always about the future marriage of the nation of Israel to the King of kings, the Son Jesus Christ. God's full intention is to have them at the center of the celebration, the exalted Bride who is the crowning glory of the Darling of Heaven. But like Vashti, they were preoccupied, and being found

busy with their own agendas, the reaction of the King was predictable and entirely in line with the history of Israel's relationship with God. Vashti is rejected as Queen, and Esther, the poor
girl rescued from the shepherd's tent, is her successor.

The second factor builds upon the first. One of the risks God
takes in being generous to His people is that there is the potential
in our hearts to become enamored with the trappings of His
grace and assume ownership of them. We tend to develop vested
interests in the side benefits of God's kindness, thinking that His
gifts are ours and that we have the right of ownership over all
that has come to us. Then, when the Lord invites us to lay some
of those things down for the sake of being about His business or
giving priority to ministering to Him, we hesitate and often simply refuse. Preoccupation with our own agenda is but the first
level of refusal. Stubbornness and flat repudiation of His desires
comes next, with angry and even violent resistance against the
Lord's initiative being the pinnacle of a closed-hearted response.

When the people respond to the King's servants by seizing
them, treating them spitefully, and finally killing them, they are
giving ultimate expression of rebuttal to the King's will. They are
saying in effect, "How dare You interrupt our involvement with
our business? We are in control, and we want nothing to do with
Your suggestions, Your parties, or Your rulership." What a tragic
set of circumstances.

Implicit in this story is yet another parable that Jesus told, in
which His foretelling of His own death is recounted in chilling
fashion. In that situation, the sending of the servants was about
examining the King's vineyards, and upon the refusal of the vine-
dressers to receive the servants, the King sends His Son, thinking
they will receive Him. Recorded in the previous chapter of
Matthew, the echo of this tale could scarcely have died down in
their minds as Jesus in effect was telling them the same story
again. Consider the climax of the account:

> **"Then last of all he sent his son to them, saying, 'They will
> respect my son.' But when the vinedressers saw the son,
> they said among themselves, 'This is the heir. Come, let us**

**kill him and seize his inheritance.' So they took him and
cast him out of the vineyard and killed him." (Matthew
21:37-39)**

The tragedy of this event is impossible to overstate. They
killed the servants, and then they killed the Son, thinking that by
this tactic they could seize the inheritance, *when it was in the heart
of the King to give them the inheritance all along!* The whole point of
relationship with the King was intimate friendship in a marriage,
and His intent was that the inheritance would be theirs. But the
people thought they had to seize it through an act of rebellion
and murder. They had been seduced as surely as Adam and Eve
and had come to a complete place of distrust in the King and
contempt for Him. The result of their hardened condition was
that they would kill the Lord of glory, the very One who would
have given them all the desires of their heart. It was a tale of
unimaginable heartbreak for them and for the King.

### The King's Response

This portion of the story is very difficult to tell because the
King's response is swift and sure. Luke's rendition, aimed more at
Gentile readers, gives us a brief summary of the unfolding events
and encompasses only the recruitment of the "whosoevers" from
the streets to fill the banqueting tables. This is the good news for
the outcasts, those who have not had a place but now are invited.
The King is in love! He has prepared a banquet to celebrate His
marriage, and you need to come, for you are the Bride! What a
wonderful declaration of hope and stunning joy. One can only
imagine Esther, standing out in the field herding a flock of goats,
suddenly summoned by her cousin Mordecai who informs her of
the dismissal of Vashti. Esther must have responded with a statement something like "well, that's too bad; but what does it have to
do with me?" Then Mordecai informs her that the Lord has spoken
that she is to be the new Queen! Talk about a paradigm shift! From
the shepherd's tent to the King's palace! I tell you, the fairy tale is
really true!

But once again, Matthew gives us the more complete story. Because his gospel is more focused on the Jewish community, Matthew gives us the full implications of the wrath of the King as released upon those who snubbed the invitation. Seen from a superficial perspective, the wrath of the King seems way over the top, completely out of proportion to a simple decision not to come to a feast. But when we understand the background, the long history of the King's initiative and appeal, the equally long history of obstinate refusal on the part of the people, we begin to see the justice of the situation.

All through the history of Israel, God had time and again given them the clear and compelling promises of His kindness and goodness. He would be for them; He would be their champion.[8] He would be their very great reward.[9] He would make them the head and not the tail.[10] He would be their Provider,[11] their Healer,[12] their Refuge.[13] He would give Himself no rest until their light shown in the darkness like a lamp on a pedestal.[14] He would rejoice over them with singing,[15] and His heart for them would be like that of a Bridegroom on His wedding day.[16]

God would serve them with tender and gentle ministrations, not being harsh, not giving them more than they could bear. He would watch over the very hairs of their head, and He would remind them of His tender mercies by showing them the stars of the heavens, lest they forget that they were His beloved.

Again and again, He would woo them; over and over, they would force Him to take drastic action. God would be forced to

---

[8]  See *2 Chronicles 20:17*
[9]  See *Genesis 15:1*
[10] See *Deuteronomy 28:13*
[11] See *Genesis 22:14*
[12] See *Exodus 15:26*
[13] See *Psalm 46:1*
[14] See *Isaiah 62:1*
[15] See *Zephaniah 3:17*
[16] See *Isaiah 62:5*

bring difficulty to their land in the form of famine and pestilence, and He would ultimately bring discipline in the form of invading armies.[17] But God had gone so far as to tell them ahead of time that all this would happen simply because they would turn away from Him.[18] All they would need to do would be to repent with genuine hearts, and He would relent from the evil He had planned and restore them to the place of His favor. The revelation of His character and mercy was great, and so therefore, the release of His judgment was severe.

### The Appropriate Nature of God's Wrath

The wrath of God being visited upon His people who refuse Him is something we don't like to think about. But the simple fact is that we must think about it, because it is a topic so clearly addressed in the teachings of Jesus concerning His Father. My goal in this book is to reveal a tender and compassionate Father who receives the broken and weary and who loves His people in an unconditional way. But it is precisely that unconditional love that will not allow them to go their own way unchallenged and unchanged. Either they will come to a place of agreement with His purposes and agenda, or they will be eliminated from His Presence, having exercised the dignity of free will in voting "no."

The offer that God makes to us of His love and care, the priceless nature of our redemption by the blood of Jesus, is so profound that it demands the right response. There can be no halfhearted answer to Him, let alone outright refusal, if we desire to be part of His Kingdom and His plan for eternity. There is no Plan B for us. It is either the life that God desires for us – a life of unimaginable glory, pleasure, and joy – or death. We are either with Him or not with Him, for Him or against Him. There are no suburbs to the City of God. We are either in or out.

God had given His people an entire history of loving initia-

---

17   See the prophecy of *Joel*, chapters 1 and 2.
18   Consider the Song of Moses, recorded in *Deuteronomy 32*.

tive that should have been enough to awaken their hearts to respond to Him. A few people did respond in the way He desired but only very few. The rest turned to their own way, despising the Lord of glory and not recognizing the day of their visitation by the Son of God. Therefore, the wrath of God was poured out upon them in the form of invasion and conquering by foreign armies. They have been removed from their land and brutalized for centuries, reaping the consequences of their refusal to embrace the Son of the King. My own conviction is that the times of difficulty are not yet passed for Israel, but that there is yet more to come as the final days of human history emerge upon us. The nation still does not recognize her need for Jesus. Her confidence is still in things other than the compassion and mercy of God, and her suffering is not yet complete.

And yet, incredibly, the door is still not closed. The Scriptures are very clear that at the end of the age, Israel will yet come to repentance. They will gaze upon the One whom they pierced. They will be visited by a Spirit of grace and supplication, their eyes will be opened, and the nation will be redeemed in a day. Their suffering will be reinterpreted as a fellowship in the sufferings of Christ, and the power of resurrection will come to them and through them. God will still have His way with His first Bride, and they will be restored to the glory of their inheritance.

### What About Us?

The primary concern of this chapter, however, is not to develop a theology of God's dealings with Israel in the times of the end. The basic question that is before us is this: what will we do with the invitation that the Father has sent out to us? Most of those who will read this book are in the category of the street people, brought into the wedding celebration because the original guests refused to come. We are the ones included purely by the grace of God, Whose desire is that all should come and not perish. We are the "whosoevers," those who are qualified for the wedding banquet simply because the King desires our presence.

We, like Esther, have been brought near by sheer grace, taken from the mundane reality of our subsistence and escorted to the King's palace to be prepared for an unimaginable life in the glory of His Presence.

What will you do with the invitation? Will you make the fatal mistake that so many have made and refuse to come because you are too busy with other things? Will you succumb to the same seductive voice that tells you that your party is better than the one He will give you? Will you politely decline like the Pharisees did, saying that you are preoccupied with other engagements?

Or, will you respond with the appropriate gratitude of one who has been plucked from the fire and chosen to be made glorious? I tell you, He has plans for you. The Father that Jesus knew intends to dress you in glorious garments that will reveal your true identity. He will exhibit you at a level of authority and power that you never even imagined could be possible. You are the King's Beloved! Leave your present pursuits, and come to the House of the King! He desires your beauty, and He will cause the nations of the earth and the principalities and powers of the air to tremble before His Bride when He puts you on display at the end of the age. Your destiny is sure. Your inheritance is certain. Your identity is glorious. All that remains is for you to say "yes" to the inviting Father.

## A Sober Conclusion

There is one sober note to end the story. As all are welcomed into the feast of the King, there is one who comes in without being dressed in a wedding garment. In other words, he has assumed that by the King's generosity he can participate in the company of the Bride without embracing the Bride's garments. This analogy refers to the cleansing process of holiness, the spiritual preparation of being conformed to the image of Jesus. There are those who seem to be part of the Bride of Christ, part of the Church, the company of the redeemed. But they have not submitted their lives to the cleansing, healing, and purifying work of the

Holy Spirit. They presume that the mercy of God means that they are welcome to stay as they are, and that God will embrace them even as they refuse the transforming grace that is provided with the invitation. God's grace, His empowering presence in our lives, inevitably leads to holiness, and when holiness is not found, grace has not been allowed to do its work.

When the King came to the celebration, He saw this one man without a wedding garment. The King confronted him, and when the man had no explanation, he was bound hand and foot and put out into the darkness. It is sober, but it is true. We shall be holy, for He is holy.

My encouragement to you is this: accept the invitation to the Father's banquet. Leave your old way of life with your own priorities and agendas. Give yourself with a glad heart to the cleansing, preparatory process of being conformed to the image of Jesus by the work of the Holy Spirit. You have been invited to be the Bride of the King's precious Son, and if you say "yes," you will be called "chosen."

## CHAPTER 9

# THE DISCIPLINING FATHER
## HEBREWS 12:3-11

Some years ago, the *Denver Post* reported a brief summary to a news story that had been developing mild interest in the Denver community for the previous several days. A young pitcher for the Colorado Rockies baseball team had been sent down to the Colorado Springs minor league affiliate a few weeks earlier, and he was none too happy about the demotion. Then, a few days later, after a poor pitching performance, he went home to his girlfriend, announced to her that she had not met his approval in some facet of their relationship, and that she therefore needed to be "disciplined." So, according to the charges filed against him, he stripped her, tied her face-down to their bed, and proceeded to lash her 15-20 times across her back and buttocks with a belt. After the completion of the "discipline," he then raped her twice. The reason this horrifying story only sparked mild interest is that this young player was only a marginal personality in the pro sports pantheon of the Denver community and as such was not awarded the fanatic attention of some more well-known celebrities.

The thing that impacted me about the coverage of this player's situation was that he used the word "discipline" to describe his brutal treatment of the girl who was supposed to be his lover. The immediate question in my mind as I thought of these two young people is this: What sort of home environment did they experience that makes it possible to commit assault, battery, and rape, and call it "discipline"? What sort of parental abuse did they endure in their respective families that served to model this kind of behavior as "normal"? What a tragic situation!

As I have taught the message of the Father's heart in numerous settings over the last 20 years, I have encountered hundreds of people who are so damaged in their understanding of discipline that it is very difficult to see the disciplines of Father God as a good thing. Invariably, those who have been physically, verbally, emotionally, or sexually assaulted in the name of discipline have to face the accompanying feelings and fears any time they are faced with a situation that involves the concept of discipline. They have to be helped again and again to separate the behavior from the person, calling the sin what it is. They must then release the offending person into the hands of a just and merciful God who desires to heal and forgive. This is the only hope that victims have of holding their tormentors in a place of mercy and forgiving them. They also must face the lies about themselves that they received as truth in the context of the abusive treatment. They then must turn away from the false self-images as seen through the eyes of their parents or other abusers and receive the true self-image that comes from a growing understanding of the love, nurture, and discipline of the Father.

This process, though painful, is essential. If we are going to understand the Father's love, we must come to understand the reality of His discipline in our lives. We must come to see the Father's discipline as the positive and truly loving thing that it is. God's discipline involves no rejection or abuse but comes to us for our good. So for this purpose I am including these three chapters on the Disciplining Father. My prayer is that in experiencing His loving discipline, you will come to know the Father's love for you as it really is.

In the twelfth chapter of the Book of Hebrews, the writer includes a section on the discipline of the Father that gives us a basis of understanding from which we can form a true perspective. It begins this way:

> **And you have forgotten the exhortation which speaks to you as to sons: "My son, do not despise the chastening of the Lord, nor be discouraged when you are rebuked by Him; For whom the Lord loves He chastens, and scourges every son whom He receives." (Hebrews 12:5-6)**

There are several things in these two short verses that set the stage for what the Holy Spirit is trying to communicate to us. First of all, this word about discipline is an exhortation, a "word of encouragement." The purpose of this teaching concerning the disciplines of the Lord is to encourage us, to fill us with strength and courage to carry on in the relationships and the tasks of the Father's house. Secondly, the word "speaks to you as sons." From this perspective, it is precisely because our sonship and daughterhood issues are settled that the Father takes us on to discipline us, to shape us into the kind of sons and daughters that will look like the pattern Son, Jesus. A true father disciplines his own children. It is a sign of relationship; perhaps even one of the most basic indicators that real fathering is taking place. The passage goes on to assert that if loving discipline is not in place, there is no sense of sonship that can emerge, but only the experiential reality of being illegitimate children.

In verse 5, we as His sons and daughters are exhorted to make right responses when we experience the Father's disciplines. Now my wife, Mary, and I have three children of our own, Dave, Alyson, and Rachel. At the time of this writing, Dave and Alyson are both married and involved in emerging careers in our hometown of Kansas City, Missouri. Rachel is nearly 15, and in her freshman year in high school, home-schooling so that she may be involved in the International House of Prayer in Kansas City, and travel with me. So we understand from years of experience that one of the great challenges of parenting is to help children understand that the disciplines that come to them are in fact a good thing. Verse 11 of our text tells us that "no discipline seems pleasant at the time," so when the child receives discipline, it is essential that be helped to see it as a good thing. The responsibility is two-fold: I must exercise discipline in a loving and godly way, and my children must make the choice to receive it as good and right.

When our son Dave was in the sixth grade, we experienced a pivotal disciplinary occasion. He had just moved into middle school and was undergoing some difficulty in making the transition from the more highly structured environment of elementary school into the experimental "open" classroom of the middle school setting. Left more to himself than he had been in earlier grades, Dave struggled with the responsibility of turning his work in on time, even though in many cases it was complete. He would simply leave it in his locker, forget it at home, or complete it a day late. In any case, by midterm his grades, which had been excellent to that point, were a disaster. After speaking with his teachers, we agreed upon a solution. Every Friday, Dave was to obtain the signature of one of his teachers on a piece of paper stating that he had turned all his work in on time. If he had not, or if he failed to get the signature, he would be grounded for the weekend. All went well for several weeks, and Dave's grades shot up to their normal level. Then, on the weekend of Thanksgiving break in late November, the worst case scenario happened. The Junior Youth Group from our church had planned a camping trip for that weekend, and Dave had been looking forward to it for weeks. However, on the last day of that particular school week, which was Wednesday, he put off getting his teacher's signature until the very last thing of the day, only to discover that his teachers were gone by the time he got to their classroom. He had his work finished, but he procrastinated a few minutes too long.

Mary and I felt terribly conflicted about what to do. Should we relent and allow him to go on the camping trip, or should we hold the line on our agreement – that was the question. Not feeling at all certain about our decision, we decided to enforce the discipline and require him to stay home. It was very painful, and

Dave struggled to accept the decision as a good one. Because our goal was discipline and not punishment, we put forth good effort that weekend and had a good time together as a family. Dave dealt with his disappointment, and what was more, became firmly established in his ability to do his schoolwork on time, with high quality. He made his decision to be trained by the discipline, to allow it to work its purposes, and not to allow his disappointment at missing the camping trip to affect our family relationships negatively. It was a strong moment in our family history.

These same principles hold true for us as children of the Father. He sends His disciplines to us for a good purpose, but it is up to us to accept that these disciplines are a good thing, meant for our well-being and not for our destruction. We therefore have several decisions that must be made if we are to benefit from the disciplines of the Lord. These choices are clearly articulated for us in the text from Hebrews 12.

The first choice we face is that we are not to "make light of the Lord's discipline." This simply means that we are to approach life with the understanding that everything that comes our way is for the purpose of making us like Jesus. We are to take that reality seriously, agreeing with the process involved. In other words, we are not to merely goof off through our lives, keeping the Father's purposes for us at arm's length. There is a verse in the hidden reaches of Psalm 119 that has given me strength in this process over the years. It says this:

**Great peace have those who love Your law,**
**And nothing causes them to stumble.**
**(Psalms 119:165)**

What this verse communicates to me is that when I love the ways of God, His Word that encompasses every situation of my life, then I can have confidence that His purposes are being worked in my heart at all times. I may need to find ways to interpret some of those situations, because sometimes they may seem to be irreconcilable with a God of kindness and love. But I've become confident through the years that with time, the Holy Spirit will make all things known to me. Therefore, I can receive all situations as the gift of God in my life, knowing that He either is providing a time of cleansing in my own heart and soul or is inviting me into a partnership with the sufferings of Jesus. I can make decisions to embrace all things, not stumbling over anything but trusting that at the end of the day, God will cause it to work out for my blessing and benefit.

The needful thing is not to make light of the Lord's discipline, not to keep the Father's purposes distant from our hearts. For some reason, the picture that comes to my mind here is my one regrettable year as a high school freshman football player. I lived in a small town in Oklahoma, and in the tiny school that I attended, almost everyone participated in almost everything. The athletes were also in the band, and the class drama productions involved everyone that was willing to participate. I loved to play basketball, but there was a clear understanding that you had a better chance of making the basketball team if you went out for football. Two things were against me: I didn't want to be there and as a freshman, I was short and scrawny. We had just moved to this town a few months earlier, and I was still the new kid, feeling very vulnerable. Because there was a crew of us that were sort of in the same boat, we found each other. The whole group of us coped with our discomfort by goofing off incessantly, despising the disciplines that, while none of us would have gotten very far in any case, would have at least helped build some character or some sense of participation in the team or something!

But the time and energy was pretty much wasted on this bunch, because we made light of the coach's discipline. As a result, the one time I was given a chance to demonstrate that maybe I had something to offer as a football player, I didn't even know what to do. My foolishness was exposed, and I missed the mark because I had not embraced the discipline set before me.

The writer to the Hebrews says, "Don't do that!" Understand that the Lord has big visions for you that go far beyond the scope of this lifetime. You have been created to look like Jesus, to act like Him, to have the same giftings and power that He knew, to be an integral part of the Body of Christ. In order to realize any of that, you must receive His disciplines, not making light of them. Make a determination today, as you read this, that you will not despise the disciplines of the Lord. Rather, take them seriously and embrace the purposes for which the Father sends them to you.

The next thing that we are warned against is that we are not to "lose heart when He rebukes you." Again, this matter of losing heart is something that is in our hands as God's children. We can count on the fact that if we receive all things as from Him, we can run to Him in the midst of our confusion and pain. We will be comforted by His Word, by the encouragement of the Holy Spirit, and by the testimony of others that have been in similar situations. Therefore, because the support systems of the Word and Spirit are always available to us, we are instructed to see the disciplines of the Lord properly, keeping a true perspective of His processes, so that we might be strengthened by them instead of destroyed.

### The Problem of Distortion

This warning would not be recorded if this were a simple matter. Because of our fallen condition as human beings, we have that thorny little problem of distortion in our perceptions of the Father as He is and of ourselves as we really are. Because of our brokenness, it is inevitable that without the proper affirmations of a father who disciplines in love, we receive discipline as rejection. We receive discipline as an indication of our displeasure to the father. I believe this to be a universal human condition that requires healing and salvation. Part of our brokenness tells us that we must earn a place as sons and daughters, that a father's love has many and often overwhelming conditions, and that discipline is a sign of the father's displeasure and rejection. The communication we receive is that we've messed up again and are farther from, not closer to, our goal of sonship and daughterhood.

But in relationship to this Father, that is the distortion and not the truth. If we knew the Heavenly Father as Jesus knows Him and if we knew ourselves as Jesus knows us, we would have no struggle with this area. We would have perfect confidence in His love for us, and therefore we would rest perfectly in His disciplines. We would see ourselves as He sees us, with perfect love and the unshakeable confidence that His love is powerful enough to accomplish His purposes in us, and we would be at peace. This is the power of Jesus' prayer for His disciples in John 17:23, that we might know that the Father loves us even as He loves Jesus. But we, as our earthly parents before us, were broken by our sinful heritage and by our own choices. Therefore, we must consistently turn away from the false thing and turn to the truth about God's love for us. This reality requires choosing on our part, and it is the main reason I have included this chapter towards the end of this book and not at the beginning. My prayer is that by now, you have begun to encounter a Father of tender mercies, of gracious love, and of great compassion. I pray that you are beginning to have a perception of God that will enable you to choose to see His disciplines in the right way.

## A Proper Understanding of Punishment

In order for us to receive His disciplines in the right way, we must come to a clear understanding of the true biblical concept of "chastening" or punishment. Our Hebrews text exhorts us to make the right choice:

**For whom the Lord loves He chastens, and scourges every son whom He receives. (Hebrews 12:6)**

Part of the difficulty we face can be resolved if we understand God's perspective of the word "punishment." In 1 John 4:18, we are told that the love of God the Father "drives out fear, because fear has to do with punishment." The particular word for "punishment" that John uses comes from the Greek word for "dwarf." It is often translated "torment" and has the implication of making someone feel small through tormenting punishment. That indeed is an awful picture, and it has nothing to do with the loving discipline of the Father that is portrayed in the Scripture.

The word for "punishment" in Hebrews 12:6 is also a strong word (it means, "to flog or scourge"), but the intent of that discipline is not to demean the child but to correct and encourage. The word picture associated with this term is that of a family servant walking with a child, perhaps on the way to school. The child wanders, due to childish curiosity, and there is a gentle correction, just a word or a touch that sets the child back on course. But if the child persists in a rebellious way, the servant carries a short stick, a "scourge," and is authorized to give a swat to the leg of the child in order to obtain the desired obedience. The writer understood that unacceptable behavior, activity that does not reflect the character of the Father, must be curtailed. If harsh measures are required, then harsh measures must be used. But there is never rejection or torment behind the correction. Rather, the goal is continuous intimacy of relationship between Father and child. Therefore, there is an understanding of a clearly defined and consistently enforced pattern of behavior that is set in place for the good of the child. Obedience to this pattern brings about a growing sense of well-being and positive self-esteem. This kind of corrective discipline is applied specifically because of the relationship between Father and child, and it is designed to strengthen and affirm that relationship, not deter it.

In fact, the writer emphasizes this idea in verse 8 when he says:

**But if you are without chastening, of which all have become partakers, then you are illegitimate and not sons. (Hebrews 12:8)**

Here the presence of discipline is presented as a normal indicator of relationship between Father and child. It is strengthened to the point of asserting that if no fatherly discipline is applied in a child's life, then the child is illegitimate, sired but not fathered, and has no true identity as a son or daughter. This is the reality of the curse that Malachi prophesied would come upon the land (Malachi 4:6) – generations of fatherless, undisciplined children who have no sense of legitimacy. Therefore, they live out their angry lives in repetitive patterns of distorted, perverted, and destructive behavior. How will they be saved? Only by being fathered, thus being brought again to a place of legitimacy and godly purpose.

## Is this Politically Correct?

I fully realize that by speaking of physical discipline – spanking, swatting, etc. – that I am being politically incorrect. However, my concern is not political correctness, but biblical discipline. I long to see the fruit of well-fathered children that stand in direct contradiction to the lawlessness that pervades the youthful elements of our society today. I am not advocating violence or abuse but a minimal enforcement of discipline for the good of the child. My children need to know that there are consequences for their behavior, and if I do not mete those out in gentle but determined ways, how will they come to know? In the absence of that kind of fatherly love, they will not feel cared for or nurtured, but rather they will feel abandoned to their own ways, left for the ravages of society to take its toll.

The matter of discipline that reinforces patterns of positive behavior for the good of the child is a key point in receiving the disciplines of the Father. Consider this statement from Hebrews 12:

**For they indeed for a few days chastened us as seemed best to them, but He for our profit, that we may be partakers of His holiness. (Hebrews 12:10)**

Here is the difference between the disciplinary motivations of the earthly father and the Heavenly Father. "Our fathers disciplined us . . . as they thought best." This statement leaves room for the real possibility of inadequacy and even distortion and perversion in the disciplines of an earthly father. Sometimes what they thought best was not best for the child, but it was in fact discouraging and even demeaning or abusive, communicating rejection instead of affirmation. Sometimes their disciplines may have been for their own convenience instead of for the good of the child. There were times when I wanted my six-year-old to go away and be quiet, not because she would have been blessed by the beauty of silent solitude, but because I was short on tolerance and patience. I remember a time when I was angry with my young son and spanked him in a way that was demeaning to him. When I finished, he looked at me and said, "Dad, that wasn't fair!" I knew he was right and immediately asked him to forgive me. Even in his childhood, he knew that there is a right kind of discipline and then there is a kind that goes beyond the boundaries of propriety. These faulty disciplines arise out of human failure, and they are thus not like the disciplines of Father God.

Rather, "God disciplines us for our good, that we may share in His holiness." The disciplines of God always have our best interests as the highest priority, that we might become like Him. His desire that we be like Him is not some perverse attempt to stifle our individuality, but that we should come to full and complete freedom and liberty as His sons and daughters. He alone is free in every dimension of His being, and thus to become like Him is to experience His freedom. The enemy of our souls would have us believe that freedom comes in resisting the disciplines of God. In fact, what results from that is the worst kind of conformity, squeezed into the tiny categories of a destructive, self-centered world system.

### Discipline as the Key to Liberty

A friend of mine who is an excellent artist was always afraid to submit fully to the will of God, fearing that such a commitment would restrict and inhibit his artistic development. He thought that obedience to God was contrary to his own development as a free person, and that he would be restricted to drawing pictures of angels on clouds or something silly like that. What he began to see was that he was projecting on God his poor relationship with a controlling father, who had always discouraged creativity and adventuresome choices. For him, the disciplines that his father thought best were not the best, but rather they served to inhibit and stunt his growth. As he forgave his dad and turned away from false images of God and of himself, he was able to see that submitting to the will of God was the only way to full creativity as an artist. God is the ultimate creative Being. He created creativity. It is His nature, and He would not discourage that in one of His children, but rather He would encourage it through loving disciplines specifically designed to maximize the potential that He placed in His child.

It is the same for each one of us. We will only find our full freedom and individuality in the context of obedience to the will of the Father, for He has our best interests at heart and knows the course we must take to be completed in what He has made us to be.

The results of the receiving the disciplines of God are magnificent. Verse 11 gives us the true perspective:

**Now no chastening seems to be joyful for the present, but painful; nevertheless, afterward it yields the peaceable fruit of righteousness to those who have been trained by it. (Hebrews 12:11)**

Discipline is not a pleasant thing. At the time it is administered, there is nothing about discipline that is enjoyable. It is only in the context of understanding the payoff that the discipline becomes endurable or even pleasant. Therefore, we must cultivate a perspective that helps us see the payoff that is coming to us as we embrace the disciplines of the Father.

In the next chapters, I want to address two different kinds of discipline that are set in place in our lives, but let me jump ahead now for just a moment. Not all discipline is corrective, that is, something to change unacceptable behavior. Some discipline is formative, designed to produce a desired end by shaping the activity of the person accepting the discipline. Anyone who accepts a formative discipline such as athletic training, musical training, or training in job skills, views that discipline with an end in mind – a championship, an excellent performance, or a well-paying job. Therefore, they see the discipline as a necessary and even good thing. Such people are even able to experience enjoyment in the disciplinary activity, because they are able to anticipate the joy at the end of the process and then to superimpose that future joy upon the present difficult experience.

When I was in seminary in Fresno, California, during the 1970s, the wife of one of the professors related a poignant illustration of this principle. This professor's family included young children at the time, and one day a little neighbor boy knocked on the door of their home. The wife came to see what he wanted, and to her surprise, the little guy asked her to spank him. Unable to comprehend the request, she invited him inside and began to search out what was behind this unusual situation. It came out that on a previous day, some neighborhood kids had been at this woman's home to play. This little boy was among them, and his behavior had been a consistent problem. That day was no exception. Finally, his actions had been so disruptive that the professor's wife had been forced to spank him to stop the undesirable activity. She then had taken him on her lap to comfort him, gently explaining her love for him. She told him that if he wanted to continue to be part of that group, he was going to have to behave differently. She held and comforted him until he was settled, and then returned him to the play activity. Some time passed, and she forgot about the occurrence until he showed up at her door asking for a spanking. She understood then that what he was craving was to be held and affirmed and comforted, and since the professor's wife was the only one who had ever given that to him, he perceived that he had to go through the first thing to get the second.

Obviously, this little guy needed a clearer understanding of the love of God, but the point is he was willing to endure the dis-

cipline for what it meant in the end – a hug and some comfort.
Our Father God gives us the same reality. There are disciplines,
both corrective and formative, that are part of being fathered.
And if we receive them, they will produce "a harvest of righteousness and peace."

Now the term "harvest" implies a multiplied increase – thirty,
sixty, or a hundred times what was planted – and that is good
news. Multiplied righteousness and peace sounds like a worth-
while investment. The variable in this verse is that this harvest is
"for those who have been trained by it." In other words, simply
going through the discipline doesn't bring the harvest, but rather
being trained by the discipline. And again, that reality is up to us.

How many of us as children endured the discipline of piano
lessons but were not trained by that discipline? That's true for
me! Now I wish I had paid attention! My son, on the other hand,
began lessons as a discipline imposed by his parents, but he
eventually embraced the process as a good thing and now has
graduated from a fine conservatory with a piano performance
degree. He is fully settled on the course of his life as a professional musician, dedicated to bearing witness to the gospel of Christ
in the world of music. He was trained by the discipline, and the
result is a harvest of blessing. In a similar way, my daughter
eventually embraced the value of disciplined activity in school. It
paid off in tremendous ways when she received a full scholarship
to the college that she had chosen. There was a harvest of blessing and righteousness.

I pray that you will set your heart to receive the disciplines of
the Father, that by them you will know His heart of love for you,
and find the fullness of His purposes for your life.

CHAPTER

# THE DISCIPLINING FATHER, PART II

# 10

JOHN 14:21-23

art of the joy of my life in relationship with the Lord is an ever-emerging appreciation of beauty. I'm learning to recognize beauty in all sorts of places as the heart of a Bridegroom God ignites my soul with passion and delight. I love to gaze on beautiful things like works of art or lovely nature scenes, but one of the most compelling examples of beauty is when some lover of God, a worshipper, presents his heart to Him in an artistic manner. Our Father loves all manner of heartfelt worship, and when the heart of worship is present, He makes no differentiation between the clumsy movements of a little child and the graceful turning of a trained dancer. God loves in equal measure the piercing tones of a tenor born to sing in the shower or the enchanting sounds of one whose song lifts the hearts of the multitude to the presence of God. But to some, God has given gifts of artistic expression, or gifts of athleticism, or gifts of intelligence that are to be refined and presented to Him in excellence and glory. He is a God of beauty, and our expressions of life are to be expressed in beautiful fashion.

The ability to express oneself with excellence doesn't just happen. It invariably involves discipline and focus, embraced for the very purpose of knowing the freedom of true creativity. I have a friend, Ruth Fazal, who is a professional violinist, and as such,

she is highly skilled on her instrument. One of the joys of my life
is to listen to her play, whether it is a solo from Bach's *Mass in B
Minor* or a spontaneous accompaniment to a poem that I am
reading. Knowing Ruth as I do, I know that the very liberty she
possesses is the fruit of the combination of wondrous gifting and
focused discipline. She has been gifted to hear the sounds of
heaven and has sovereignly been given the ability to play, but her
skill of performance has come through untold hours of rigorous
discipline in the solitude of the practice room. Without that, there
is no true beauty released. Every true artist knows this is so. In
addition, the truth is that the more Ruth gives herself to the
development of excellence so that she can play what she hears,
the more she is allowed to hear. Faithful with what she has been
given, she is given more.

And it is no different with the rest of us. God has designed
each one of us for excellence and virtuosity in living our lives
before Him. It is in the embracing of the Father's disciplines that
these life-skills emerge. My hope in this chapter is to introduce
you to the formative disciplines of God set in place to release us
into all the glory He has for us in this life and the next.

Our text in Hebrews 12 introduces the topic in this way:

**If you endure chastening, God deals with you as with sons;
for what son is there whom a father does not chasten?
(Hebrews 12:7)**

What does the formative discipline of God look like? The text
goes on to tell us that discipline is hardship, not pleasant, and
even painful, but that by its very nature it produces desirable
things in us if we receive it.

In this chapter, I want to examine the first of two broad categories of discipline that can help us gain perspective on the situations of our lives as children of the Father. First, let me reiterate a
basic assumption that arises from an understanding of Psalm
62:11-12, which reads as follows:

**God has spoken once, twice I have heard this: that power belongs to God. Also to You, O Lord, belongs mercy; for You render to each one according to his work. (Psalm 62:11-12)**

My assumption, based not on some wish or dream but on the unshakable reality of His Word, is that God is loving and that He is strong. In other words, He has the desire and the ability to direct my life in a way that is for my best. The Father is not capricious in these attributes – they are central to His nature. He cannot deny them, nor can He act in a manner inconsistent with or contrary to them. He will not decide on a whim to treat me in an unloving way. Neither will He ignore my need nor somehow be rendered incapable of doing what is best for me. Nothing is out of His control, and He is careless about nothing that concerns me. He is strong and loving, and that is all I need.

Because of this, I can rest assured that any event or situation that comes to me, no matter how difficult, can be placed in the category of hardship received as discipline for my benefit and ultimate blessing. Because He is strong, I am confident that no situation is outside His ability to be victorious. Because He is loving, I am confident He will speak to me concerning the situation, and He will let me know what is being formed in me or what needs to be corrected. He is not a Father who makes us crazy with unexplained, whimsical disciplines, but One who gently leads us, even through times of great difficulty. He is a loving, strong Father. This understanding is foundational to comprehending and receiving the Father's disciplines as good.

Out of His strong, loving nature comes His discipline, and I find it expressed in two primary ways – His formative disciplines and His corrective disciplines. Let's examine them in that order.

### The Formative Disciplines of the Father

Every family has significant dates that mark the history of their lives together, and one of the dates that is important for the Wiens clan is August 12, 1986. That date is inscribed in the corner of the concrete slab that served as the family basketball court, roller hockey practice field, tanning salon, and whiffle-ball arena during the years we lived in Colorado.

It was early in the summer of 1986 that we decided to construct this area next to our garage. It was a waste spot, covered with weeds and grass, really just a mound of useless dirt hidden away behind our front fence and not visible from the back porch. But David and Alyson wanted a basketball court, and I had promised that we would build one there. So we labored long hours, pulling weeds, hauling out yards of excess dirt, building a four-foot high retaining wall so the neighbor's fence wouldn't collapse and generally preparing the area for its intended use.

Now I am not an expert in the art of construction with concrete, but I do know that it is not functional to simply call the cement company and ask for a load of concrete to be delivered. Preparations have to be made before the concrete arrives, and then once it is poured, a lot of hard work remains to achieve the desired results. Through this process of construction, I wished many times that I could just speak a command and have a basketball court materialize. In actuality, I realized that without the work, all I would have would be a mound of concrete where the dirt had been; no more functional, just harder and more expensive.

So we prepared the area, making certain it was level, with just the slightest angle for drainage purposes. We laid reinforcement rod across the length and width, forming a steel grid that would provide strength and permanence to the court. Then we constructed a form out of boards in the precise dimensions that we had in mind for the court. We waited for a nice day, arranged for some help, got the wheelbarrows, shovels, and hoes lined up, and then called the concrete people. They came and dumped the concrete in the prepared place, and we worked like dogs for several hours to push the mud into all the corners, to level it, to smooth it, so that it would be what we intended. Because the concrete was still wet and soft, we could shape it into the exact form provided by our structured preparations, so that we knew at the end of the process, we would have the basketball court we desired.

Then, just as we were admiring our work, a Colorado summer rain storm blew in, and we found ourselves scrambling to find a piece of plastic big enough to cover the wet concrete, lest it wash away in the rain and all our time, energy, and money be spent in vain. With all of these processes and near catastrophes finally finished, at the end of the day we had a pretty good basketball court shaped and formed. The last step in the process was to allow the cement to cure, to fully harden so that the stresses of usage wouldn't cause cracks and decay. So we let the court sit unused for three days of August sunshine, and then it was ours to use to the fullest degree.

The point here is that in order to be usable, the concrete had to be formed by some external factors that were not part of the finished product. The form is not the basketball court, but it is essential to the formation of the court. Without the form, the court could not have been built; after the court hardened into its intended shape, the form was no longer necessary.

Formative disciplines are like that in the lives of God's sons and daughters. They do not constitute the life of the individual, but they shape that life into the desired reality so that it may exercise the purpose God intended it to have. The writer of the Book of Proverbs spoke about the formation of a life:

**Train up a child in the way he should go, and when he is old he will not depart from it. (Proverbs 22:6)**

Another way of translating that verse could be:

**"Train up a child according to his bent, and when he is old he will not turn from it."**

My understanding here is that in the heart of God the Father there is a pattern and a purpose for every one of us as His children. He knows the details of each person's makeup, and He is the source of each personality. Each human being in some way reflects a facet of the Father's nature and character, and thus he has a unique place in the Father's heart. Couple this reality with the fact that God is a speaking God, a communicative Father who cares enough about the development of each person that He will speak about them to anyone who will take the time to listen. The primary vehicle of this formative process is the Word of God. In Galatians, Paul tells us of the formative function of the Law of God:

**Therefore the law was our tutor to bring us to Christ, that we might be justified by faith. (Galatians 3:24)**

The purpose of the Word of God is to form a pattern for our lives to guide us to Jesus Christ. The sense conveyed here in the Greek language is that of a "child-conductor." This was a family employee charged with walking alongside the children, seeing that they stayed on the proper course until they reached their destination. Once the child was old enough to make right decisions and take responsibility for himself, the child-conductor could be released. This is the value of building habits of studying and meditating on the Word of God in the life of the young believer. These habits escort us into the Presence of Jesus through the use of external markers until we come to a measure of maturity in our faith. Then the Word ceases to be merely restrictive; instead, we internalize the Word, it is written on our hearts and becomes the chief avenue of the direction of Christ in our lives. When we read it or study it, we interact not merely with rules and regulations but with our Lord Himself.

The second tool that is primary in the formative discipline of the child of God is people, specifically our family members.[1] In our particular family, both my wife and I come from a long her-

---

[1] I want to remind you that for those whose family does not function in godly ways, the Lord Himself takes them up, placing them in holy relationships in the Body of Christ.

itage of music and worship. Our parents, although raised in different states, were from the same Mennonite Brethren tradition that was rich in choral and instrumental music. For both of us in our separate environments, part of the rite of passage into adulthood was to begin singing in the church choir as soon as we graduated from the eighth grade. We had monthly Sunday night programs, which served as the training ground for young musicians to present their instrumental and vocal talents before the church so that this heritage could be passed along.

Therefore, when we had our own children, one of the first things we determined was that they were going to have music lessons from childhood right through their teen years. This was our commitment as parents to our children. It arose out of the conviction that we needed to provide for them the opportunity to excel in something that was consistent with our family values and priorities. The reason I say this decision was our commitment to our children is that children, at the age of five or seven or even twelve years, do not have the ability to make ten to twelve year commitments. They function in much shorter time frames, and we knew that if we left it up to the kids, they would choose not to continue the first moment it became difficult.

We chose the Suzuki method of piano instruction because it is geared to young children and emphasizes two things that we think are important. First, it stresses playing melodies before learning theory, much as we learn to speak before we learn proper grammar. Second, this method stresses parental participation in both the lesson times, as well as the practice sessions. So for ten years during the time that our older two children took lessons, we went with them every week. We observed the lessons, jotted notes on the instructions given by their teacher, and then sat with them at their practice sessions, supervising them as they worked out their assignments. At first, the reality was one of rote learning, the children simply playing notes they had heard on a recording, mimicking the sounds of another's performance. We played the songs for them, one phrase at a time, asking them to repeat what they had heard. We formed their hands into the proper shapes and positions. We helped them sit straight. We found, through simple trial and error, the best motivational strategies, the best practice times, the proper balance of reward and consequence. We listened to scales tens of thousands of times, and most importantly, *we did it because we love them and desire the best the Lord has for them.* This was not about torture, but about formation – shaping the skills and the character of our children, giving them tools that would be transferable to every area of their lives. It gave us many opportunities to work out the details of our relationship, forgiving one another, growing in patience and tolerance, slowly bringing to our children the reality of loving, formative discipline.

I will never forget the day, about five years into David's development, that I came downstairs to listen to his practice session. He was already playing, and as I approached, I suddenly stopped and stood still. David had been working on a Rachmaninoff prelude, and he loved this piece. As I paused at the top of the stairs, I realized that he was no longer merely playing notes, but that he was making music. He was intent over the keyboard of our old upright piano, and was passionately engaged with Rachmaninoff's soul, pouring everything that he had in his nine-year-old self into that music. Something had awakened inside him. He was no longer a kid taking piano lessons; he had become a musician. I wept as I listened, knowing that a transition had taken place, that David had touched something eternal, and that my heritage had become his inheritance. He would never stop making music.

The same thing happened with Alyson, only it came via the flute instead of the piano. Although she followed the same regimen as David, with the same teacher and the same methods, Alyson was never able to connect spiritually with what she was doing until she began to play the flute. It was as though she needed a different domain than her brother. Music was her heritage, but her bent was slightly different. She was not a clone, but her own person, and it has been through the channel of studying and playing the flute that she has become a worshipper. In later years, as she played with our worship team, the lilting melodies carried the congregation into the Presence of the Lord. She learned to improvise, so that the songs of heaven that transcend the notes on a page would flow from her instrument as she prophesied unto her heavenly Father.[2]

These processes of discipline are so important because freedom is the result of formative discipline. Without it, our lives are not free, but merely chaotic. A young or undisciplined child may sit down at a piano keyboard and begin to play spontaneously and creatively, but what emerges is not music, but chaos. We have mistakenly come to the conclusion in our culture that what our children need is freedom of expression, but unless formative discipline is part of the equation, what will result will only be chaos, not beauty.

Rachel has also engaged the process of the formation of her musical abilities. Although we gave her piano lessons as we did the others, it became clear to us early on that she was a singer. Even as a little child she sang constantly, making up her own songs of joy and lament, processing truth as she understood it, processing her emotions and hurts, giving expression to the life that was forming within her. She now sings on worship teams at the International House of Prayer in Kansas City, and there is a prophetic edge that is emerging in her walk with God. This seems to be her bent, and we will train her in it accordingly, that she might find the path that is there for her to travel. My favorite Rachel song for all time went something like this: "I am not a boy, I am not a cat, I am not a dog, I'm a girl!" It was great!

## Formation Produces Disciples

The point of sharing these stories is this: If we, as imperfect earthly parents, can provide formative discipline that produces good fruit in the lives of our children, how much more does our heavenly Father do the same for us and perfectly so? The term

---

[2] See *1 Chronicles 25:1*

Jesus used for the men who followed Him most closely was "disciples." The term is the same as the word "discipline" and implies a relationship that consisted not only of friendship and camaraderie but also of formation. Perhaps the first thing Jesus said to the three men who would form the nucleus of His small group was about this formative process:

> **And as He walked by the Sea of Galilee, He saw Simon and Andrew his brother casting a net into the sea; for they were fishermen. Then Jesus said to them, "Come after Me, and I will make you become fishers of men." And immediately they left their nets and followed Him. When He had gone a little farther from there, He saw James the son of Zebedee, and John his brother, who also were in the boat mending their nets. And immediately He called them, and they left their father Zebedee in the boat with the hired servants, and went after Him. (Mark 1:16-20)**

The purpose of Jesus in the lives of His disciples was to form them into the very men God had created them to be. The transformation of these men from impetuous, volatile fishermen into mature, empowered servants of God would involve the process of being discipled. They needed to be formed into the image God had in His heart long before He gave them life. For me, the Gospel accounts in the New Testament have taken on an entirely new dynamic since I began to see the stories as the record of the training, formative process in the lives of the followers of Jesus. Two stories in the New Testament, one in the Gospel of Matthew and the other in the Book of Acts, serve to illustrate the point.

The first text is found in Matthew 17 and is the story of when Jesus instructed Peter to go fishing and pay the temple tax that was due for the two of them. When this encounter is interpreted as an exercise of formative discipline in the life of Peter, it takes on a whole new meaning. The text reads as follows:

> **When they had come to Capernaum, those who received the temple tax came to Peter and said, "Does your Teacher**

**not pay the temple tax?" He said, "Yes." And when he had come into the house, Jesus anticipated him, saying, "What do you think, Simon? From whom do the kings of the earth take customs or taxes, from their sons or from strangers?" Peter said to Him, "From strangers." Jesus said to him, "Then the sons are free. Nevertheless, lest we offend them, go to the sea, cast in a hook, and take the fish that comes up first. And when you have opened its mouth, you will find a piece of money; take that and give it to them for Me and you." (Matthew 17:24-27)**

In this story, Jesus primarily gives an instruction about who is liable for the taxation laid upon them. He then assigns Peter to do a very strange thing. He tells Peter that a miraculous event is awaiting him, but that he is going to have to do something risky and apparently foolish in order to realize the miracle.

For some reason, much of Jesus' teaching to Peter centered around the fishing industry. Peter was an expert in that field and had looked to that profession as his source of income and livelihood. So Jesus and Peter had squared off more than once in this arena – the overwhelming catch of fish after Peter had fished all night without success, the multiplication of the fish to feed the 5,000, to name two such events – and now He was doing it to Peter again. I believe that Peter needed to learn the Lordship of Jesus in Peter's own area of expertise, so that he would fully be able to trust the Father for his provision and well-being, and he would no longer have confidence in his own human ability.

So Jesus tells Peter to go fishing and that the first fish he catches will have a four-drachma coin in its mouth, with which he can pay the temple tax for him and the Lord. Picture Peter's response: "Lord, You want me to do what? Look, I've been a fisherman for my whole life and, first of all, I'm not going fishing with a line off the pier. That's what tourists do, the guys with cameras and black socks and Bermuda shorts. I'm a professional; I work with boats and nets. Secondly, I've never seen a fish with a coin in its mouth. Why do you want me . . ." and Jesus cuts him off in mid-sentence: "Peter, are you my disciple?" "Yes, Lord.

Okay, okay, I'll go. But this beats everything I've ever seen."

Can you see Peter walking down the road toward the lake, muttering to himself: "This is the stupidest day of my life." John sees him going and shouts:

"Hey Pete, where you headed?"

"I'm going for a walk."

"Can I go with you?"

"I'd rather be by myself."

Peter gets to the water and says, "I can't believe He's making me do this. Are you the fish, or is it that one over there?" He throws his line in, pulls out the fish, opens its mouth, and has a Pentecostal experience. "Bless God, I knew it! I knew that I had the faith! Jesus said it, I believed it, and that's enough for me!"

And the fact of the matter is Peter did believe *because he did what Jesus said to do.* He was trained by the discipline in his own area of expertise, and the result was a new understanding of the power and grace of God. The next time Jesus would ask him to do something strange, he would have more faith to do it, because he had been formed in faith by the disciplines of the Lord.

The second story is recorded in the Book of Acts, and it has to do with the raising of Tabitha from the dead. Here is the text:

> **At Joppa there was a certain disciple named Tabitha, which is translated Dorcas. This woman was full of good works and charitable deeds which she did. But it happened in those days that she became sick and died. When they had washed her, they laid her in an upper room. And since Lydda was near Joppa, and the disciples had heard that Peter was there, they sent two men to him, imploring him not to delay in coming to them. Then Peter arose and went with them. When he had come, they brought him to the upper room. And all the widows stood by him weeping, showing the tunics and garments which Dorcas had made while she was with them. But Peter put them all out, and knelt down and prayed. And turning to the body he said, "Tabitha, arise." And she opened her eyes, and when she saw Peter she sat up. Then he gave her his hand and lifted**

**her up; and when he had called the saints and widows, he presented her alive. And it became known throughout all Joppa, and many believed on the Lord. (Acts 9:36-42)**

This is an incredible story, and one that must have firmly established the authority of God upon Peter in the eyes of those who witnessed this miracle. What we tend to do with this kind of account is chalk it up to the unique gifting of Peter and wish that such power was available today. But if you recall the story Jairus' daughter being raised from the dead by the hand of Jesus in Luke 8, you will see that Peter was trained in the ministry of the miraculous just as we must be trained and formed to do the work God has called us to do. Read the text:

**When He came into the house, He permitted no one to go in except Peter, James, and John, and the father and mother of the girl. Now all wept and mourned for her; but He said, "Do not weep; she is not dead, but sleeping." And they ridiculed Him, knowing that she was dead. But He put them all outside, took her by the hand and called, saying, "Little girl, arise." Then her spirit returned, and she arose immediately. And He commanded that she be given something to eat. (Luke 8:51-55)**

Notice the remarkable similarities that occur in these two stories. In both cases, the person was dead when the Lord's servant arrived on the scene. In both cases, there were professional mourners already in place, along with family and friends. In both cases, these extra people were removed from the room in which the corpse was laid out. In both cases, the servant took the person by the hand and commanded them to "get up." In both cases, the revived person was presented to those who were awaiting the results.

It seems clear that Peter had learned from his experience of the ministry of Jesus to the daughter of Jairus. Later, after Jesus had left the earth and released the power of the Holy Spirit upon the Church, when Peter went into the room where Dorcas lay, he must have thought, "You know, I've been in a situation like this before. Now how did Jesus do this? Oh yeah, the first thing is to get rid of all these people. Now let's see, what next? Okay, take her by the hand. Well, maybe I'll pray first. All right, now what did He say? Oh yeah, 'get up!' Praise God, He did it again!"

Peter was formed in his ministry through his relationship with Jesus Christ. He learned how to pray, how to preach, how to work miracles, how to cast out devils by standing next to Jesus as He did those things. Formative discipline marked the boundaries that Peter was to walk in and that would shape him into the empowered servant that God had in mind when He gave Peter life.

It is the same today with us. God places us in relationship with those who will form us and shape us in the things that He has in mind for us, and He will also give to us those whose formation we are to oversee. This begins in the family and continues in the Church, providing for each of us relationships and assignments that give meaning and focus to our lives from our first years to our last. In the early years of my life in ministry, it was my privilege to come into relationship with two men, Blaine Cook and Bob Jones. These men were used by the Lord in my life to form me in the ministry of the gifts of the Holy Spirit. I learned how to pray effectively for the sick by standing next to Blaine, watching people get well under his hands. He would instruct me in where to place my hands and in what to say, and I saw people touched by the power of God. I learned how to speak the word of knowledge and the word of prophecy into the lives of people by standing next to Bob Jones as he spoke. I observed the amazement on the faces of the people as he told them of things in their lives he could not have known except by the Holy Spirit. I saw them weep and rejoice as the grace of God touched and empowered them to go on in their walk with Him. Then these men, each in their turn, released me to minister on my own. They encouraged me to take the risk of hearing the word of the Lord myself, to dare to step out of the boat and walk with the Lord in the realm of the supernatural. Today, my greatest delight is not only in ministering these things, but in training others who stand alongside me, imparting to them the skill to use the gifts with which they have been endowed by the Holy Spirit.

On many occasions I have been sitting in a public place, like a restaurant, and have observed someone come in to sit at a nearby table or booth. Suddenly, I sense that I know them, and can see in their faces something of the character and purpose of God. I have learned that when that happens, I am in the midst of a moment of formative discipline, and I have the choice whether to be trained by it or not. I have learned to obey those impulses, to speak by faith the things I sense the Holy Spirit speaking to my heart – just a thought, or a simple word-picture. I have seen the blessing of God come to people through my obedience, and the joy that accompanies the discipline is worth the risk.

Allow me to cite one example of this kind of encounter. Some time ago, a family – husband, wife, and three daughters – walked into a restaurant where I was seated with two friends, and sat in the next booth. Something in my spirit knew they were believers, and I sensed wisdom in the man, and a spirit of encouragement in the woman. So I got up from my place, and introduced myself to the family, asking if I could share something with them. After confirming that they were indeed believers, I spoke the things I had sensed in my heart concerning them. This, I believe, involved the gift of word of knowledge and the presence of discernment, gifts that are available to any believer, since the Holy Spirit, Who is the source of the gifts, resides in every believer. As I spoke to them, the man and his wife affirmed that what I was saying was accurate, and then the sweetest thing happened. One of the daughters, who looked to be about 10 or 12 years old, looked at me with the most tender smile and said "You just received a message from heaven for us!" They were encouraged and I was blessed to be the vehicle of that encouragement.

I believe God the Father has that sort of experience for each of us, many times over. The key that opens the door to the ministry of Jesus through us in the power of the Holy Spirit is formative discipline. Those who are trained by it reap a harvest of righteousness and peace, and walk in the joy of the Lord's Presence. My prayer is that you will know this joyful thing as well.

## Redefining Hardship as Discipline

There is one other dimension of formative discipline that must be considered, and that is the reality that is spoken to us in Hebrews 12:7, where we are instructed to "endure hardship as discipline; God is treating you as sons". This is a difficult verse to comprehend because in our performance-oriented society, we have come to the conclusion that if we do right, things ought to go well for us. We mistakenly think that difficulty ought not to be present unless we have missed the mark somehow. This perception has been encouraged by certain approaches to teaching in the Body of Christ concerning faith. These approaches suggest that if we have appropriate faith, say and do the right things, that life will be heaven on earth, a utopia of green lights, thorn-less roses, material gain, and spiritual power. The only problem with this approach to life is that it does not fit within the framework of the whole counsel of Scripture. We are instructed clearly in both Old and New Testaments that hardship comes to us not only to correct us and point out things in our lives that must be fixed. Hardship also comes to faithful, obedient sons and daughters that they might be conformed to the image of Jesus, and demonstrate that faithfulness and obedience before the watching world.

While Hebrews 12:7 could be interpreted to only mean corrective discipline (we'll get to that in Chapter 11), there is no mistaking the fact that a passage such as James 1:2-4 refers to the formative, proving blessings of difficulty. Consider the words of the brother of our Lord:

**My brethren, count it all joy when you fall into various trials, knowing that the testing of your faith produces patience. But let patience have its perfect work, that you may be perfect and complete, lacking nothing.
(James 1:2-4)**

The Greek word translated "trials" in verse 2 is *peirasmos*, which is defined in Strong's Concordance as "a putting to proof by experiment, by the experience of evil; by implication, adversity." In verse 3, the original word translated "testing" is *dokimion* and has the meaning of "probing, or putting to the test." What is being put to the test in these verses is faith itself. Some Christians would have us believe that if we have proper faith, we will not undergo tests at all, but that is simply not true. Hardship comes to the believer to probe our faith, to test the faith that has been growing, and to see if it will stand up under pressure.

In Isaiah 64:8, the prophet uses the word-picture that the people of God are like clay in the hand of the Master Potter. He shapes us and molds us as He wills, and then, as any potter knows, the freshly formed vessel is placed into the fire to prove its worth. This is to see whether any defects will be exposed or whether it will be proven a finished vessel, ready for use in the Potter's house. The skillful formation of the vessel does not eliminate the need for the fire; it simply ensures that when the fire comes, the vessel will be proven worthy.

To my mind, the best example of this reality in the Old Testament is the story of the three young men in the Book of Daniel. Recorded in Daniel 3, this familiar account reveals nothing about these three young men that could be considered sin or lack of faith in their lives. Living in Babylon during the captivity of Judah, Hananiah, Mishael, and Azariah (whose names were changed to Shadrach, Meshach, and Abednego), along with Daniel, are considered the best and the brightest because of the favor of God upon their lives. They are in fact so faithful that when the pagan king demands their allegiance, they refuse, knowing full well that death in the fiery furnace awaits them. When their decision is challenged, the three youths respond to the king in the following fashion:

**Shadrach, Meshach, and Abed-Nego answered and said to the king, "O Nebuchadnezzar, we have no need to answer you in this matter. If that is the case, our God whom we**

**serve is able to deliver us from the burning fiery furnace, and He will deliver us from your hand, O king. But if not, let it be known to you, O king, that we do not serve your gods, nor will we worship the gold image which you have set up." (Daniel 3:16-18)**

The king becomes so angry that he orders the furnace heated seven times hotter than normal and has the young men thrown in. The fire is so hot that the slaves who carry the youths to the furnace are burned to death in the process. But once inside, not only do the three survive but "one like the Son of God" shows up to accompany them in the blaze! Their faith didn't keep them out of the test; rather, their faith was demonstrated in the test!

Hardship demonstrates our sonship for the real thing that it is. Hardship exposes our faith in its real condition. If the fire reveals a flaw in the vessel, the potter begins again. However, unlike the natural potter, the Master Potter, who is our Father, does not discard the flawed vessel, but He softens us with His love and reforms us until our worthiness is demonstrable.

Jesus, of course, is the New Testament model of this reality. The fact that the Sonship of Jesus was proven by hardship is revealed in Hebrews 5. Consider the text:

**who, in the days of His flesh, when He had offered up prayers and supplications, with vehement cries and tears to Him who was able to save Him from death, and was heard because of His godly fear, though He was a Son, yet He learned obedience by the things which He suffered. And having been perfected, He became the author of eternal salvation to all who obey Him, (Hebrews 5:7-9)**

The death of Jesus was a suffering experience that came to Him so that He might learn obedience and become the source of our salvation. Now does this text imply that Jesus was ever *not* obedient or that He was ever *not* the source of our salvation? Of course not. Jesus was always obedient and was always the source of our salvation from before the foundation of the world. The text means that His obedience had to be demonstrated in the context of real suffering so that His Sonship could be proven and unquestioned.

Our loving Father does the same with us. He allows testing to come, not so that He will know whether we will be faithful, but so that we will know our need and experience His grace and mercy in that time. The Father has always been confident of the power of His love to meet us in our places of need. Consider the attitude of the Apostle Paul toward difficulty:

> **For I am persuaded that neither death nor life, nor angels nor principalities nor powers, nor things present nor things to come, nor height nor depth, nor any other created thing, shall be able to separate us from the love of God which is in Christ Jesus our Lord. (Romans 8:38-39)**

### The Father's Testing Policy

The tests come so that in passing them, we will come to know that we have been made faithful by the power of the Holy Spirit, and we have been confirmed in our full inheritance as His children. If we break down during the tests, and our faith is shown to be immature, then we experience His love and restoration as He picks us up, holds us, comforts us, and prepares us for the next proving. If we live in the proper understanding of the Father's disciplines, we will be encouraged by them. His testing and proving method is fail-proof. He always gives "open-book" tests; you can go to the Scriptures at any time and find other saints in history who have been examined in the same way. He allows us to talk with our friends during the testing time and gain understanding from them about how to go forward. He allows us to ask questions of Him during the test, and He will provide all the answers if we're willing to trust and wait. And finally, He allows us to keep taking the test until we pass. His testing policy is fail-proof! It is the way of the Father, and it is good.

So, with the writers of Scripture I say to you, do not be over-

whelmed that you are required to face difficulty and hardship.
God is treating you as His child. For when you enter the test, His
Son will walk with you in it. When you have completed the test,
His nature and character will be fully formed in you, that you
might know the full joy of your inheritance as a child of the
Father.

# THE DISCIPLINING FATHER, PART III
## HEBREWS 12:5-6

# 11

**A**nd though the Lord gives you the bread of adversity and the water of affliction, yet your teachers will not be moved into a corner anymore, but your eyes shall see your teachers. Your ears shall hear a word behind you, saying, "This is the way, walk in it," whenever you turn to the right hand or whenever you turn to the left. (Isaiah 30:20-21)

One of the most comforting realities of the Father's House is that of a present Father who will not neglect us, who will not allow us to fatally stumble and accidentally ruin our lives. He will not ignore us and let us foolishly make wrong choices to such a degree that they will cause us to miss that for which God has created us. Rather, as I stated in the previous chapter, the Father watches over us in every moment, and from time to time, He allows us to encounter situations of testing and proving, that we might come to see what is inside our hearts and minds.

One of our great failings as human beings is that we insist on having a better perception of ourselves than we ought to have. C.S. Lewis points out in his classic book *Mere Christianity* that,

**When a man is getting better, he understands more and more clearly the evil that is still left in him. When a man is getting worse, he understands his own badness less and**

**less. A moderately bad man knows he is not very good; a thoroughly bad man thinks he is all right. ...Good people know about both good and evil; bad people do not know about either. (p. 87)**

So when our Father allows us to face testings that are designed to prove us, we are faced with seeing ourselves as we are. When that happens, the Father speaks into our lives about any changes that need to take place. This is the process of corrective discipline. If we are quick to respond to Him, the corrective discipline is not much different than formative discipline. He desires that we be quick to repent, quick to change our minds and our behavior, and quick to receive forgiveness, mercy, and the power of the Holy Spirit to grow up and act differently. But the fact is that our natural response is to think more highly of ourselves than we ought to think. Therefore, we tend to resist the formative disciplines of the Lord and continue on our own way. It is then that the corrective disciplines come into play with more clarity and precision.

In the matter of raising our own children, it quickly and surprisingly became apparent that our little wonders had minds of their own. We saw early on that it was easy for them to set those minds on various courses of action that sometimes did and sometimes did not conform to what we as parents thought was best. When those courses of action seemed to us as unwise or unhealthy, we would take steps to change those courses. We chose to apply the least amount of pressure possible to gain the desired correction. But we quickly learned that there are times when only pain will bring about the desired change in attitude and behavior.

Our son Dave had been walking for a couple of months when this reality became clear to us. As a young couple in the 1970s, our stereo equipment, though modest by any measure, was important to us. So as Dave learned to toddle, we quickly got tired of saying "No!" when he got near the stereo or the TV, and we put barriers up. Sofa pillows, extra chairs, and the bench from the dining room set were sufficient to keep the equipment beyond his arm's reach, and we thus established an external barrier that more or less ensured his compliance with our desires. But as we all know, external compliance and internal compliance are not necessarily the same thing.

One night we had dinner guests, and the barricades had to be cleaned up. Everything was fine until Dave had finished eating and wanted to get down from his chair. I put him down on the floor, and he immediately headed straight for the television set. We adults were engaged in conversation when suddenly the room exploded with sound as Dave simultaneously pulled the "on" button and cranked up the volume. He fell backward on his bottom as the noise startled him, and we all laughed at the sight. I went over, turned off the TV, picked Dave up to comfort him in his fright, and gently said, "No, don't do that, okay?" There was no punishment needed, for he was merely being curious. Children should never be punished for being curious. That's how children are supposed to be, and it is how they learn. To punish a child for curiosity is to stifle them and wound their spirit, which is a tragic thing to do.

But now I had introduced the law: "Don't do that." Now there was a standard, and the issue would no longer be curiosity but obedience. I set Dave down on the floor, and again he headed straight for the TV. We watched in amazement as he got to his destination *and then turned toward me to make sure I was watching!* Then he pulled the button, cranked the volume, and laughed out loud! He had seen us laughing the first time, and the anticipated pleasure of the activity and of our response outweighed any fear of the noise or any influence my "don't" statement had upon him. So, because he had, in Dr. James Dobson's words, "flopped his big hairy toe over the line" and was now directly disobedient, the correction was much stronger. I went to him again, turned off the TV, picked him up (no laughter this time!), and looking straight into his eyes said "I told you 'no'! Stop that, or I will spank you!" Again, the anticipated pleasure was greater than the fear of the threat, and the moment I set him down he repeated his actions, waiting for me to watch before he pulled the knob.

As I held my son in the aftermath of the spanking, comforting him in his pain and in the sudden realization that his actions had consequences, I told him how important it was to obey me. I reinforced the truth that learning to obey me would keep him safe and protected until he was old enough to make his own decisions about his life. Had I not followed through on this, I would not have fulfilled my responsibilities as his father, and Dave's understanding of his sonship would have been in question.

Alyson learned "no" in a different way. She liked to play with the electrical outlets, and between the time that we discovered that and said "no" and the time we were able to buy those little plastic guards that fit in the outlets, she stuck tweezers in one and got knocked on her rear end with a good jolt! God protected her in our carelessness, and she got the message in a hurry: "Don't play with the outlets!"

However, it is our daughter Rachel who provided us with one of the best stories of development in the disciplinary process. When our children were young, we embraced the strategy of counting to "three" as an early warning system that if a change of behavior did not occur immediately, there would be drastic consequences. "One" meant this: "I'm really serious about this; I want you to stop what you're doing." "Two" meant, "You are on the verge of big trouble, and you need to stop NOW!" "Three" meant it was too late; the line had been crossed, not by curiosity but by rebellion, and corrective discipline was immediate.

One night, when Rachel was about three years old, we had put her to bed, and Mary and I had settled in to watch a little TV before we went off to sleep. Suddenly, we became aware of this "presence" behind us, and we turned to see Rachel standing there, waiting to be invited to join us. So, feeling generous, I beckoned her to come and sit between Mary and me on the love seat we were occupying. She came and stood in front of us, and calmly told us to get off the couch, that she wanted to sit there. I was somewhat startled, and said, "No, Rachel. There is plenty of room. Come sit between us." She replied again that she wanted the sofa to herself, and I let her know that was not going to happen.

In the next moment, the most amazing thing occurred. Rachel looked me in the eye and said "One!" My three-year-old was counting me out! Mary and I burst out laughing in stunned amazement, got down off the couch, and gave her the place she wanted. That kind of brazen prayer needed to be answered.

Rest assured, we had many other situations where we did not give in to her, but that one was something special.

## Discipline is for Our Good

Because God is a good Father, He treats us as a father does his children, only without carelessness or irritation. He never disciplines us for His convenience but only for our good (Hebrews 12:10), with our best interests in His mind, and the development of our holiness as His goal. So the first step in His disciplinary process is to set the boundaries. He did it with His very first children, Adam and Eve, when He said to them:

**You are free to eat from any tree in the garden; but you must not eat from the tree of the knowledge of good and evil, for when you eat of it you will surely die. (Genesis 2:16-17)**

Here is the very clear delineation of what is acceptable and what is not. Now in order to have a true love relationship with the Father, a relationship of voluntary love, the children had to have the opportunity to choose not to have that relationship. A relationship without choice cannot be love but merely robotic. The Father does not desire puppets but children who love Him, and therefore they must have the opportunity not to love Him, to choose not to have relationship.

Therefore, the stage was set for the drama of Genesis 3. Desiring voluntary love from His newly made children, God intentionally withdrew His tangible, immediate Presence from them so that any choice made would be fully of their own choice.

So when the enemy came as the serpent and enticed them, Adam and Eve deliberately chose to disobey, and then were faced with the consequences of their behavior, namely, separation from God and the introduction of death into their lives. Now this separation was not rejection by God. Rather, it was for their protection, since to be in the Presence of Holy God is to be given totally over to holiness. Any sin in the life of the individual would be fatal in God's immediate Presence, not because He is intolerant, but because holiness and sin cannot coexist. So God removed them from His pure Presence so they would not be destroyed, and He immediately set in motion the system of payment for sin through sacrifice. He did this by killing an animal to provide covering garments for His wayward children and by promising them that one day He would deal with the enemy by crushing his head under the heel of the woman's offspring, namely, Jesus.

So throughout the record of Scripture we can discern this pattern: God takes initiative with His children to establish relationship. He gives them life and everything they need to live. He establishes behavioral boundaries and the means to live and move within those boundaries. He articulates clearly the consequences of going outside the boundaries, and He establishes ways of returning to relationship once the boundaries have been violated.

I must underscore again the reality that there is only one option for gaining life and all the blessings and rewards that go with it. In our culture, we can choose to live at various levels of experience that on a comparative scale look relatively positive or negative. We can be really healthy if we don't eat fat and if we exercise every day. We can be moderately healthy if we live in moderation in all things. Or we can be unhealthy if we insist on maintaining a bad diet, living with loads of unresolved stress, ingesting poisonous substances like drugs or too much alcohol, and so on. We like to be able to choose the relative level of our existence.

But when the question of eternity is posed, when it comes to choosing life over death, we must see that there is only one option. If we want life, then it is going to be in relationship with God on His terms. If we choose not to accept those terms, then the result is not a reduced quality of life, but it is death. Moses recorded these options accurately as he wrote the words of God in the Book of Deuteronomy:

> **See, I have set before you today life and death, good and evil, in that I command you today to love the LORD your God, to walk in His ways, and to keep His commandments, His statutes, and His judgments, that you may live and multiply; and the LORD your God will bless you in the land which you go to possess. But if your heart turns away so that you do not hear, and are drawn away, and worship other gods and serve them, I announce to you today that you shall surely perish; you shall not prolong your days in the land which you cross over the Jordan to go in and possess. I call heaven and earth as witnesses today against you, that I have set before you life and death, blessing and cursing; therefore choose life, that both you and your descendants may live; that you may love the LORD your God, that you may obey His voice, and that you may cling to Him, for He is your life and the length of your days; and that you may dwell in the land which the LORD swore to your fathers, to Abraham, Isaac, and Jacob, to give them. (Deuteronomy 30:15-20)**

What is clearly presented here is that God has given us as His children explicitly defined parameters for living that are founded upon a love relationship with Him as our Father. The desire of His heart for us is articulated in the last phrase of verse 19 and in verse 20. There it is made clear that we are to love God, listening to Him, and obeying Him because He is our life, and any reward we hope to gain is in Him. There is no other option for life but loving and obeying God. There is no Plan B. I have encountered many who say, "Well, if that works for you, that's fine, but I choose to live differently." The problem with that response is that there is no other choice that involves life. The only other choice is for death. This is not because God is a punitive, self-centered

deity that exacts revenge on those who don't see things His way.
That is the style of the Greek, Roman, or Norse gods of mytholo-
gy who were in fact demonic in their nature. The reason that God
our Father is so clear about choosing life or death in relationship
to Himself is that He alone is life. Outside of relationship with
Him, there is no life. Not just different life; no life. Remember the
statement of John the Gospel writer in John 1:4 – *"In Him* **(the
Word, or Jesus) was life, and that life was the light of men."**
Life is in Him alone, and the parameters that He has established
are for the purpose of describing what characterizes that relationship.

That sounds like bad news, but it really is not. Although in
one sense the Gospel is very restrictive (life according to the way
of the God of the Scriptures or death), the thing that makes it all
good news is the reality of the Father's love for all people. His
love is so all-encompassing that He has taken initiative with
every person to reveal Himself, to show the way to relationship
with Himself. He has given entry points into that relationship so
that every individual can freely make the choice to love Him or
not. [1]

## God's Kindness is Not Mere Sentiment

What the love of God does not do is to declare blanket
amnesty regardless of the quality of relationship with Him.
People of our time do not understand the loving nature of our
God. They think of Him as a "good God," but what they have in
mind is a benevolent, doddering old fool that is more like a senile
grandfather than a God whose love is strong and holy. They
think that because He is gracious, He will merely smile at them,
say, "Well, children will be children," and let them go on in their
craziness because "after all, He is good, and a good God would-
n't send anyone to Hell."

---

[1]See *Romans 1:18-32* for the New Testament perspective on the universal nature of God's self-revelation.

That is not the God of the Scripture. His love is such that it requires relationship, for love without relationship is not love, but mere sentiment. True love desires the best for the object of that love – true freedom and true happiness – and will do everything in its power to see that this true freedom and happiness is attained. God's love is a determined love, a love that will set us free, even if He has to change our very nature to accomplish His goal. If we choose to respond to His love, He will move heaven and earth to make it possible. And yet, if there are those who are determined to resist that love, even though their resistance is paid for with eternal death, God will not force Himself upon them. In the language of C.S. Lewis – "He cannot ravish; He can only woo."

Therefore, when God chose the nation of Israel as His own and determined that it was through this nondescript little collection of tribes that He was going to bring His kind of love to the whole world, He set in place the Law. This was the system of guidelines that would direct His people toward Himself and that would reveal to them their dependency on Him for the ability to live according to His nature. In a relationship of intimacy with Him, they would find the grace to become like Him. His character would become theirs, His nature would be theirs, and His Kingdom would be theirs. Even when they failed, He would point to a sacrificial system set in place before the creation of the world. This prophetic system would find its fulfillment in the life, death, and resurrection of Jesus. It would ensure by the power of the Holy Spirit that God's people would be fully formed in His character. In this way, the relationship of intimacy with His people that had always been His plan and goal would be realized, and the God and Father whose love is higher and deeper and wider and longer than any created thing would have the relationship of love with His people that His heart had always desired.

God's desire was to make certain that His people would stay close to Him or would return to Him after periods of wandering. Therefore, God instituted corrective disciplines, consequences for rebellious behavior that would serve to turn their hearts back to the Father whose desire was to bless them. He informed them that if they remained close to Him, their lives would be characterized by blessing, provision, and protection at every turn. But if they chose to turn to their own way, He would allow and even send consequences upon them that would drive them back to Him for forgiveness and restoration. What we must see is that these consequences come precisely because He loves us and is determined that we be free.

## The Promise of Blessings and Curses

The basic instruction of God to His people is found in Deuteronomy:

**Hear, O Israel: The LORD our God, the LORD is one! You shall love the LORD your God with all your heart, with all your soul, and with all your strength. And these words which I command you today shall be in your heart. (Deuteronomy 6:4-6)**

Following these introductory phrases is a long list of positive blessings and benefits that would come to the nation of Israel as they learned to love God with all their hearts. Then, in Chapter 8, verses 19-20, Moses records the statement of warning concerning disobedience:

**Then it shall be, if you by any means forget the LORD your God, and follow other gods, and serve them and worship them, I testify against you this day that you shall surely perish. As the nations which the LORD destroys before you, so you shall perish, because you would not be obedient to the voice of the LORD your God.**

When the people walked with God, they experienced the incredible blessings and power of His hand guiding them, fighting for them, providing their needs, and generally caring for them and loving them. But when they turned from God, becoming enamored with the ways of the surrounding nations who did not acknowledge God, then God would allow the corrective disciplines to come into play. They would experience defeat in battle where before there was only victory. They would experience sickness where before they walked in health. They would experience famine where before the crops had been consistently bountiful. They would experience the social ills of the surrounding pagan societies where before there had been holiness and blessing.

It is important to see that God was consistently patient in the release of these disciplines, preferring to allow the Israelites to simply experience the fruit of their own waywardness and turn back to Him. This was His strategy in relation to the prodigal son in the story told in the first chapter of this book. Often, the trouble we get ourselves into is sufficient to turn our hearts back to the Father, and He is patient enough to wait for self-imposed trouble to have its effect. However, God is determined to have His people for Himself. In time, motivated by His great love and commitment, God would even be forced to loose the murderous power of pagan nations upon His own people, hoping to drive them back to Himself. In Isaiah 10:5 God calls the nation of Assyria *"the club of my wrath,"* which He extended as a disciplinary tool against Israel. In the 29th chapter of that prophecy, the Lord God lays out a chilling scenario in which His disciplining Presence is embodied in the physical enemies of Israel, as He desires to use a military siege to turn His people back to Himself:

**I will encamp against you all around, I will lay siege against you with a mound, and I will raise siegeworks against you. You shall be brought down, you shall speak out of the ground; your speech shall be low, out of the dust; your voice shall be like a medium's, out of the ground; and your speech shall whisper out of the dust. Moreover the multitude of your foes shall be like fine dust, and the multitude of the terrible ones like chaff that passes away; yes, it shall be in an instant, suddenly. You will be punished by the LORD of hosts with thunder and earthquake and great noise, with storm and tempest and the flame of devouring fire. The multitude of all the nations who fight against Ariel, even all who**

**fight against her and her fortress, and distress her, shall be
as a dream of a night vision. It shall even be as when a hungry man dreams, and look – he eats; but he awakes, and his
soul is still empty; or as when a thirsty man dreams, and
look – he drinks; but he awakes, and indeed he is faint, and
his soul still craves: so the multitude of all the nations shall
be, who fight against Mount Zion. (Isaiah 29:3-8)**

The miracle is that even though the Lord Himself wages war
on His own people through their enemies to cause them to
repent, the moment they even mumble to Him from the dust He
comes to their rescue to destroy their enemies and make their difficulties seem like a mere dream. The purpose for all this activity
was always to turn the hearts of Israel back to their Father, that
they might enjoy the benefits of His love once again.

The history of God's people in the Old Testament is the
record of a downward spiral from holiness and power to ungod-
liness and captivity. The decline lasted several hundred years,
solely because God, in His patience and long-suffering, would
restore blessing to the nation at the slightest hint that they were
turning back to Him. He gave them the benefit of the doubt in
every circumstance, repeatedly sending spokespersons to the
nation in the form of prophets and prophetesses whose function
was to remind the people of their commitment to love God and
follow Him. They would warn of the consequences of rejecting
God's love, and although there were occasions in which the people responded positively, the overall reaction was to reject the
prophets and continue in their descent into godlessness. Yet
throughout the decline, God's invitation to return to Him was
made clear in passages such as 2 Chronicles 7:14, where the Lord
says:

**If my people, who are called by my name, will humble
themselves and pray and seek my face and turn from their
wicked ways, then will I hear from heaven and will forgive
their sin and will heal their land.**

All the Father required was that they would turn to Him again, rejecting their self-centered lifestyle, humbling themselves and acknowledging their need. Then He would turn back to them, forgive them, and restore them to the place of blessing that had been theirs at the beginning.

It is no different for us today. The laws of God are still in force. His grace and power have been purchased for us through the life, death, and resurrection of Jesus Christ. This enabling power has been released to us who believe through the indwelling Presence of the Holy Spirit, and it empowers those who trust Him to live according to His ways. But those who turn their backs on Him continue to reap the consequences of their activity. In Galatians 6:7-8, Paul writes the New Testament equivalent of the Deuteronomy statements of blessings and curses:

**Do not be deceived, God is not mocked; for whatever a man sows, that he will also reap. For he who sows to his flesh will of the flesh reap corruption, but he who sows to the Spirit will of the Spirit reap everlasting life.**

God is still calling all people to Himself, and as He always has, He uses every means at His disposal to do so. When we see the ills of our society expanding in epidemic proportions, we can be sure the voice of God is in the midst of it. He is inviting every person to turn to Him, to call out to Him, even if that call is only a mumble in the dust. Scourges like disease, poverty, child abuse, and war certainly have their origin in our enemy, the devil. But where Satan would desire to kill through those means, God desires that those experiencing the "club of His wrath" would turn to Him and find comfort and release. Ever since the shocking events of September 11, 2001, we have seen the increasing activity of the Lord releasing the hand of an enemy against America. The sad thing is that we continue to put our trust in technology and weapons of war, instead of turning in repentance to the God who would heal us in a moment if we gave Him the chance to do so.

## My Own Story of Corrective Discipline

Tragically, many who have never known Him in the beauty of His love and holiness blame Him for the very consequences of their own choices that released the hatred of the enemy upon their heads. I am personally just a few years removed from the most severe period of corrective discipline I have experienced in my 50-plus years of life. The Vineyard church that my wife and I planted in 1983 had prospered in a moderate way. We had grown to around 700 people in attendance, with a small staff of six associates and support people, and I had developed an expanding schedule of conferences centered around the restoration of God's people to Him as their Father. Unfortunately, I neglected to take care of those in my own church who needed fathering. Although my own family was doing well, I was unwittingly relating to my church leaders in the same style as my own father had related to his leaders many years earlier. I stopped giving attention to the leaders of the congregation, neglecting their needs, refusing their counsel, and calling my personal whims the leading of the Holy Spirit. Although I was warned repeatedly by people who cared about me, so that I am without excuse, I did not heed the warnings, and during about a three-year period, some unresolved conflict began to fester in the hearts of a core of the leadership people.

The conflict grew to be a cancer that affected the whole leadership team of the congregation, about thirty people. When gentle appeal had no effect on me, they became the "club of God's wrath" in my life, and the church began to disintegrate. The collapse seemed agonizingly slow, covering about a year from the time we first began to address the issues forcefully. By that time, the hurt had turned to anger, and it slowly became apparent that the church would not survive.

The lowest point came for me in August of 1992. It had become clear that the church was going to die, and I had gone to the mountains to the cabin of a friend for a personal retreat, to try to gain some perspective and hopefully hear a comforting word from the Lord. As I arrived at the cabin and got my stuff arranged, I took out my Bible and turned to the devotional reading that was on my schedule for that day. It began with Jeremiah 30:12-15, and the words of God hit me like a multi-megaton blast:

> **For thus says the LORD: "Your affliction is incurable, your wound is severe. There is no one to plead your cause, that you may be bound up; you have no healing medicines. All your lovers have forgotten you; they do not seek you; for I have wounded you with the wound of an enemy, with the chastisement of a cruel one, for the multitude of your iniquities, because your sins have increased. Why do you cry about your affliction? Your sorrow is incurable. Because of the multitude of your iniquities, because your sins have increased, I have done these things to you."**

With a voice that was fairly a shout, God was letting me know that this crisis in my life was from Him, brought on by my own deeds of neglect and the abuse of authority over the lives of His children. The instant I read the words, my own anguish boiled over, and I began to weep and cry out to God in repentance and remorse. I had been under siege by the hand of the Lord, and from the rubble and dust, I mumbled my cry for help, and in His mercy, He heard me.

After some time of digesting this passage, which seemed to carry only judgment and no hope, I felt impressed to read on. It was then, in verses 16 and 17 that I felt the embracing arms of the Father Who disciplines and then restores as He spoke to me once again:

> **"Therefore all those who devour you shall be devoured; and all your adversaries, every one of them, shall go into captivity; those who plunder you shall become plunder, and all who prey upon you I will make a prey. For I will restore health to you and heal you of your wounds," says the LORD, "Because they called you an outcast saying: 'This is Zion; no one seeks her.'"**

That is the nature of the corrective discipline of our Father. He calls things as they are, and He lets us know that our sin is such that it can only bring death to us. And yet, somehow, in His mercy and love, He lifts us out of the shame of the consequences and loves us again, and in His own time restores to us the blessing of His hand. Although the consequences for my failure as a pastor were great, yet He used them to draw me to Himself, so that my confidence would be found in Him alone. He wanted to accomplish something in my heart and character that was necessary for me to be conformed to the image of Jesus. He allowed me to continue pastoring for a season, and He surrounded me with a group of faithful men and women who have spoken the truth in love to me. Among that group of friends, I have been given another chance to work out the dynamics of relationship at which I failed before. In recent years, He has allowed me to move into the purposes for which He created me in the first place. All has been restored, and I say with confidence and joy that God is a gracious Father, and that His disciplines have brought about the fruit of righteousness to this one who has been trained by them.

He is a Father who means to have relationship with us. He means for that relationship to be holy and just. His character will not be compromised, but neither will His love. He will do what is required for us to love only Him, that we might become truly free. He is a good Father, and by His disciplines, we come to truly know ourselves as His children.

CHAPTER
# THE GIVING FATHER 12
LUKE 12:32

The thesis of this book is very simple. Most Christians believe that the Scriptures teach that God is a loving God; however, many of us have not experienced the love of God in a way that profoundly touches us in our innermost being. There is a major difference between knowing what the Bible says about the love of God and experiencing the touch of His presence in a deeply personal and intimate way. King David, in his wonderful meditation on the love of God that is recorded in Psalm 36, speaks of the experience of God's affections in picturesque and emotional language that is beyond the knowledge that most of us have:

**How precious is Your lovingkindness, O God!**
**Therefore the children of men put their trust**
**under the shadow of Your wings.**
**They are abundantly satisfied with the fullness of Your house,**
**And You give them drink from the river of Your pleasures.**
**For with You is the fountain of life;**
**In Your light we see light.**
**(Psalms 36:7-9)**

Now there is a picture of intimate and joyous experience – drinking from the river of the pleasures of God! My question is this: is your experience of God such a dynamic thing that you have to create poetic language to describe it, or is it something less than that? Do you know what it is to have a Heavenly Father that enjoys you, that experiences delight concerning you even in your immaturity, and whose priority it is to communicate that delight to you in tangible ways?

My guess is that for most of us, it would be more like this. I have three children, and let's imagine that when they were small, I would write love notes to them. Perhaps I would tuck the love notes under their pillows or put them into their lunch boxes so that at school they would find the notes. And these notes would say something like this: "I want you to know how much I love you! You're the best! All my affections, Dad."

Sounds good, right? But what if I never saw them, never got down on the floor and played with them, never held them in my arms and kissed their cheeks? I could write them letters every day, and they could read those letters and come to a certain understanding that, "Boy, Dad loves me! He leaves me a letter everyday!" But in terms of the experiential reality of this love in their heart, they are not going to know that I love them unless I spend time with them. They need me on the floor with them, snuggling and wrestling, hugging and kissing, and disciplining and spending time, listening, touching, and being together. There is a difference; there is an added dimension between understanding the love and the character of the Father at an intellectual level and experiencing Him in our heart.

My belief is that there are many of us who long for the touch of God's love, but who simply do not expect that it will ever be our portion. We perceive that what God wants from us is holiness, faithfulness, dependability, generosity – all the character traits that are in fact descriptive of the spiritual life of the Believer. But we don't expect to be on the receiving end of any of those things in terms of what we receive from God. At best, we hope that we will avoid irritating Him, so that He will not withhold the things we need for daily existence, and so that He'll let us into heaven when we die.

The fact of the matter is that the Bible portrays God in a very different way from the caricature I have just described. The

Father that Jesus knew is a generous, open hearted God who is filled with joy at the prospect of communing with His children. He is a Father who delights to give them the blessings of His nature and His abundance. So, in this chapter, I want to focus on The Giving Father, to explore what the Scripture says about the liberality that is so much a part of who He is. I believe that as we begin to see Him as a giving Father, we will position ourselves to receive from Him with more confidence and expectancy.

## God's Willing Generosity

In Luke 12, Jesus is speaking to His disciples about confidence in God's ability and willingness to provide the things we need for basic, daily life. He then contrasts that confidence with the matter of worry. Worry and anxiety are twin residents in hearts that are underdeveloped in their sense of God's bigness and goodness. They are the attending demons of a small soul, one that has accepted responsibility for life, but has missed out on the magnificent kindness and limitless power that our Father has available for us in the boundless resources of His grace. Jesus was addressing such issues in the lives of His disciples, and spoke these words:

> Then He said to His disciples, "Therefore I say to you, do not worry about your life, what you will eat; nor about the body, what you will put on. Life is more than food, and the body is more than clothing. Consider the ravens, for they neither sow nor reap, which have neither storehouse nor barn; and God feeds them. Of how much more value are you than the birds? And which of you by worrying can add one cubit to his stature? If you then are not able to do the least, why are you anxious for the rest? Consider the lilies, how they grow: they neither toil nor spin; and yet I say to you, even Solomon in all his glory was not arrayed like one of these. If then God so clothes the grass, which today is in the field and tomorrow is thrown into the oven, how much more will He clothe you, O you of little faith?

**"And do not seek what you should eat or what you should drink, nor have an anxious mind. For all these things the nations of the world seek after, and your Father knows that you need these things. But seek the kingdom of God, and all these things shall be added to you.**

**"Do not fear, little flock, for it is your Father's good pleasure to give you the kingdom. Sell what you have and give alms; provide yourselves money bags which do not grow old, a treasure in the heavens that does not fail, where no thief approaches nor moth destroys. For where your treasure is, there your heart will be also."**
**(Luke 12:22-34)**

The phrase that gives me a key to this passage is found in verse 32 – *"do not fear, little flock, for it is your Father's good pleasure to give you the kingdom."* That is a massive statement! We are not to be fearful because our Father will give us His Kingdom, and it is His good pleasure to do so! He is the giving Father, and He enjoys what He does! Because of that reality, we can live in a carefree way, with liberality of spirit and confidence of heart. We can escape the anxiety that plagues those who are filled with a sense of responsibility but have no sense of the availability of the Father's resources. We can focus our attention on real things, things of the Kingdom of God, being confident that everything we need and even desire is provided through His gracious generosity.

I did a little Bible study on this matter of the giving nature of God, and there was so much material I had to settle on only a few highlights. One could easily write a whole book just on this topic, but I will focus on a few points of God's openhandedness that speak powerfully to me and hopefully to you.

Let me first of all set the context clearly. In the Luke 12 passage, Jesus is speaking directly concerning the matter of material needs and provision. He is exhorting His disciples to put an end to their patterns of worry and anxiety over their daily needs and to rest in the Father's loving and certain care. Again, this sounds

wonderful to us, but in my experience as a believer, most times
that I've heard this text taught, it has been in the form of a rebuke
to the listeners, instead of a celebration of God's bigness. We find
anxiety in ourselves and in one another, and we urge one another
to deal with our anxious feelings and to eliminate worry from
our lives. The focus is on my need to deal with my anxiety, and
the result is that I feel more anxious about dealing with that broken place in my heart! The truth is that I have never been able to
successfully deal with the problem areas of my own soul unless
there was a compelling and beautiful reality that stood over
against my fear.

I'm reminded of the story of the prophet Elisha and his servant that is told in 2 Kings Chapter 6. The king of Syria is trying
to attack Israel, but God's revelations of the king's activities come
to Elisha, and the attacks are foiled again and again. So, in frustration, the king sends a great many chariots and horses to sur-
round the city in which Elisha is staying, in order to deal with
him. When Elisha's servant sees them, he is beset with fear.

Now if that servant were a contemporary Christian, someone
might exhort him to face his fears and overcome them, or someone might sell him a book on fear management, or yet another
someone might criticize his lack of spirituality for daring to
admit that he was afraid. Elisha, though, had no criticism for the
young man's emotional condition. Anyone who saw the armies
of the enemy surrounding the city would feel the same way,
*unless* he could see compelling evidence that this was nothing to
be afraid of. So when Elisha urged him not to be fearful, he did
not appeal to the young man's personal resources. Rather, he
invited him to see reality. Then, Elisha asked the Lord to open the
young man's eyes that he might see things as they really were –
the armies of heaven surrounding the enemy were infinitely
more in number and in power. The reality that dealt with the servant's fear was solely based in the revelation of the superior
power of God and His angels, present with the situation fully in
control.

If we are going to deal successfully with the anxiety and

worry of our lives, it will not be because we are spiritually disciplined enough not to think about the troubles around us. That is unrealistic and irresponsible. Rather, we are called to focus our minds and hearts on the way things really are, on the bigness and generosity of God, and His delighted willingness to give to us all that we need, simply because He likes us! When we have first-hand experiential knowledge of a Father who loves us, who enjoys our presence and whose pleasure it is to give us His kingdom, then we find worry and anxiety melting away with no effort on our part except the effort required to focus our minds on Him.

## My Own Story

As I have shared previously, for some years I was occupied as the senior pastor of a somewhat successful Vineyard Christian Fellowship in Aurora, Colorado. When the church was three years old and had grown to about 500 adult attendees, the favor of the Lord was on us in some significant ways. It was a time of prosperity in Spirit and in material things, and I thought I was well on my way to fame and fortune as a humble servant of God. (That's kind of what I always wanted to be – rich, famous, and humble!!)

As an individual and as the leader of this congregation, I had collected a stack of prophetic promises of what the Lord wanted to do in my life and in our area, and it was a rather impressive list. I had no idea there would be serious testing, pruning, and anguish as the Spirit of God would begin the process of forming me into the suitable partner He desires me to be. But as I would spend time considering these promises, praying over them and trying to figure out how to make them happen, I found myself becoming more and more anxious. Though I was unaware at the time of the inaccuracy of this belief, I understood those promises to be a job description, an assignment from God for which I was responsible and for which I would be held accountable at the end of the day. I thought I had to do this thing for God in order to

attain His affection and approval, and my problem was that I
didn't know how to go about producing the things He had spoken about.

This sense of inability produced an anxiety in me that resulted in a great deal of pain for many people. My leadership style
became coercive as I would try to get people to do what needed
to be done. Relationships suffered and waned because the completion of the task was weighing heavily on my soul. I didn't
know how to produce what was being called for, and the weight
of that burden caused much difficulty for me personally and for
all those involved.

During that season, the Denver area Vineyard pastors had a
fellowship day, a time for worshipping together, ministering to
one another, and encouraging one another in what God was
doing among us. As I sat in the worship time that day, a clear
and potent picture emerged in my mind. I saw a small boy sitting
in the middle of the floor with a large and complex toy sitting in
front of him. It was one of those construction project toys with a
million pieces and instructions that might as well have been in
Latin. At any rate, this little guy was clearly feeling that he was
supposed to build this toy, and he had no clue how to begin,
much less how to complete it. It was way over his head, and yet
he felt the weight of responsibility. I began to share that picture
with the other pastors, and as I spoke, emotion began to flood
my spirit, and I started to weep. This was not one of those tender,
teary moments of experiencing God's affections; this was a tidal
wave of emotional overload that burst forth, and I simply melted
down in front of God and everyone else.

Tom Stipe, who was the Regional Overseer of the Colorado
Vineyards during that time, said to me, "Gary, the word is for
you," and that just compounded the issue. Several friends came
over and began to pray for me, and as they embraced me and
prayed, I saw another part to the picture. In the second install-
ment, my father came to me, put his arms around me, and said,
"Would you like me to help you with that?" Then he took me on
his lap and began patiently and kindly to explain what to do

next. And I began to see. The Father's purpose in giving me these things to do was not because He needed help. Rather, it was for the purpose of building a context for intimacy and friendship around the task. His desire was for me to give myself fully into His care, and see the ministry develop as He would show me what to do next. The anxiety in my heart began to melt away, not because I was "gaining the victory," but because I was feeling the strength and wisdom of the Father's presence as He gave me what I needed in order to do with Him what He had promised.

It took some time for me to get hold of this reality, and the following years included a major "death" experience, the collapse of my church and a long process of healing and restoration.[1] But the seeds of truth were being planted, and God's infinite patience was fully engaged as He waited for me to come in a real way to that place of intimacy to which He had invited me that day. My testimony is that during the intervening time, God has shown Himself faithful in being the Father I need, the Father who is pleased to give me His Kingdom and show me how to live with what He has given.

## WHAT THE FATHER HAS GIVEN US

When Jesus made that startling statement in verse 32 of our text, declaring that it is the Father's good pleasure to give us the Kingdom, what did He have in mind? I want to take the next few pages and outline just a few of the things that are clearly made available to us in the Word of God concerning what has been provided for us by this giving Father.

### His own Son, Jesus

Perhaps the most famous verse in all the Bible is John 3:16, where Jesus Himself is speaking to the seeking Pharisee, Nicodemus. Jesus references the Father's great love for human beings and informs this questioning elder that because of love,

---

[1] This story is more fully told in Chapter 11 of this book.

God gave His only Son for the redemption of all who would open their hearts to believe in Him. Lost in the familiarity of this passage is the massive, overwhelming reality that the Father's main gift is Himself, in the person of His Son! This is not just childhood memory verse trivia; this is the centerpiece of all biblical doctrine and experience. We are so loved by God that His first and foremost gift to us is the gift of His own life, embodied in the person of Jesus, that we might have intimate relationship with Him for all time and eternity.

Dr. Karl Barth, one of the most brilliant Protestant theologians of the 20th century, was once asked to share the most profound truth he had encountered in the decades of study to which he had given himself. Expecting some profound and lofty theological formulation, the questioner was surprised to hear Barth's answer: "Jesus loves me. This I know, for the Bible tells me so."

In the eighth chapter of his letter to the Romans, the Apostle Paul makes a stunning declaration as he strengthens the hearts of the believers in Rome on this very issue of dealing with anxiety:

**What then shall we say to these things? If God is for us, who can be against us? He who did not spare His own Son, but delivered Him up for us all, how shall He not with Him also freely give us all things? (Romans 8:31-32)**

What Paul is saying to the Romans and to us is that if God has already given us Jesus, what would He possibly hold back? Since there is nothing more valuable to God than the life of His Son, and since the Father decided that we were worth that purchase price, how could we possibly think that He would withhold such things as daily provision, or protection, or wisdom, or spiritual power, or anything else?

Furthermore, Paul goes on to say that since the Father paid that price, how can we think He would just let us slip through His hands unnoticed, stolen away by some unexpected strategy of the evil one? Rather, he dials up the reality that nothing, *nothing* is going to take us out of the Father's hand – not accusation from the enemy, not persecution, not famine, or tribulation, or distress, or peril, or sword, or nakedness – nothing! He has given us His Son! How can we be afraid that He will let us go?

O, Beloved, there is such vast comfort in musing upon the truth that God has given us His Son, Jesus. This is no small thing. It is the first thing, and really the only thing. Jesus is a gift motivated by incalculable love, a passion-driven gift, an exorbitant gift, and the fact is our Father was glad to give Him in exchange for us. He was delighted to purchase us as His children forever, so that He might in turn give us to Jesus at the end of the age as the perfectly prepared Bride made ready for the Son who is worthy!

## The Holy Spirit

Because of who Jesus is, His disciples loved Him as they had never loved anyone else. Though they were weak in their humanity, their hearts deeply desired to be with Him always. I can only imagine what it must have been like to look into those eyes, to see His kindness and affection, to feel the touch of His hand as He encouraged and exhorted, as He taught and healed. My heart surges with longing even as I write this, for there is nothing that fills me with yearning more than to think about seeing Jesus face to face.

Because of this attachment to Him, there was great pain in the hearts of these men and women as Jesus began to speak to them of going away. They couldn't imagine what life would be like without Him. His love had absolutely transformed their lives; they would never be the same, and the idea of facing life without His presence was beyond their ability to comprehend.

But Jesus gave them hope. He knew that He was going to give them a gift, a present so profound, a gift so amazing that He could actually say to His dear friends, *"It is to your advantage that I go away . . ."* (John 16:7). Imagine that! Jesus promised to His friends that He had something in store for them that would be better than His physical presence! While this seems astonishing to me, I have to remember that I'm writing this chapter as one who has received that gift from the hand of the Father. This gift is the Holy Spirit, who comes to live inside us and to minister to us from within that we are the Beloved of God, the perfect Bride-in-waiting for His perfect Son.

Jesus called the Holy Spirit "the Helper," for He would come alongside us and help us to know the truth, to remember who we are. He would help us by speaking to our hearts from the inside, bearing witness with our spirits that we are the Father's children. He would strengthen us with might in the inner recesses of our being, touching us with the affections of Jesus, healing our hearts, refreshing us in times of weariness. He would teach us everything that we need to know, the truth of our identity and destiny, the richness of our inheritance in Christ. He would take eternal wealth from the storehouse of Jesus' heart and make it known to us. He would bind us together with other believers in unity and peace, and He would comfort us with the knowledge that it won't be long until we see Jesus again.

This gift of the Holy Spirit stands right alongside the gift of Jesus as the most precious gift imaginable, and He comes from the hand of the giving Father. It is stunning to think about – God has arranged things so that as I open my heart to Him, His own Spirit will come to live inside me. He will enable me from the inside out to know Him, to follow Him, and to wait for His return. It is by the presence of the Holy Spirit that we are empowered to do the things that have been prepared for us to do, for He comes as the Spirit of wisdom and understanding. By His presence, we know how to live, for He is the Spirit of counsel and knowledge. Through His indwelling, we have the ability to do what is necessary, for He is the Spirit of might, and by His attendance, the delightful fear of the Lord fills our hearts, causing us to tremble before the Father as we kiss the Son we love.

Oh, the gift of the Holy Spirit is a wondrous reality!

**The Gift of Sure Mercy**

One of the most astoundingly beautiful passages in all of

Scripture is found in Isaiah 55, where the prophet declares the
kind and merciful intentions of the Lord as He calls His people to
Himself. The powerful poetry of this text has wondrous impact
on the human heart as it pronounces the immeasurable tenderness, patience, and kindness of the heart of God toward those
who will come to Him. Consider verses one to three:

**Ho! Everyone who thirsts, come to the waters;
And you who have no money, come, buy and eat.
Yes, come, buy wine and milk without money and without price.
Why do you spend money for what is not bread,
And your wages for what does not satisfy?
Listen carefully to Me, and eat what is good,
And let your soul delight itself in abundance.
Incline your ear, and come to Me. Hear, and your soul shall live;
And I will make an everlasting covenant with you --
The sure mercies of David.**

Could there possibly be a more gracious passage written in
the language of men? Isaiah is pronouncing over us the very
Word of God that declares His focused intention to release abundant mercy on anyone who will come to Him. He will profoundly bless anyone who will hear His voice and feast on the profligate provision of His heart of love. And the phenomenal truth is
that this is not just a one-time offering. He intends to give the
bountiful supply of His mercies to us in an everlasting way,
under the classification of "the sure mercies of David."

In God's assessment of David's life, recorded in Acts 13:22,
the heavenly conclusion that is drawn is that David was "a man
after God's own heart," who did "all My will." Now if you've
spent any time at all reading the life of David in the Old
Testament, you know that this guy was as weak as anyone! He
broke every commandment there is to break, had seasons of deep
darkness and compromise, and lived in the midst of trouble all
his days. But the thing that set him apart from every other king
in the Old Testament was David's unrelenting confidence in the
kindness of God, expressed to him even in the lowest places of

depression and fear. Something had gotten settled in his heart. It was the knowledge that even in his weakness, God liked him and enjoyed him. Therefore, he could easily confess sin and run to the Father's arms the moment he realized what the problem was.

This confidence in God's kindness[2] endeared David to God's heart. The Father had given David the promise of "sure mercy," and David took Him up on it. The wonderful pledge given to us in Isaiah 55 is that if we will approach the Lord, He will give to us that same commitment, that same everlasting covenant – the covenant of sure mercies.

The Isaiah text tells us that anyone who is thirsty may come and partake of this promise. The announcement goes out from the prophet's mouth that whosoever is willing to come may find their needs met in His presence. He strengthens the argument by asking why anyone would make the choice to eat and drink from other sources, when the real Source is freely available! We were created to eat and drink life from this Source; why on earth would we go somewhere else and try to nourish ourselves from that which is not real food or real drink?

He then gives us the practical pathway to this place of nurture: *"Listen carefully to Me, and eat what is good."* The answer to the cry of the thirsty heart is in the place of intimate relationship with the Father, drawing near to hear Him, to listen to His voice, and thereby to be strengthened by His love. There is delightful abundance there, and for those who will come, for those who incline their ear to Him and listen, God promises that they will receive the everlasting commitment of His heart to flood them with mercy at every turn – the sure mercies of David.

You see, the Father is after one thing from you – intimate relationship. When He sees that your heart is turned to that place in response to His wooing, He does everything in His power to facilitate the relationship. He makes Himself available through the written Word of God, causing it to come alive as we meditate

---

[2] See *Psalm 18* for a wonderful summary, written in response to God's deliverance from evil during a time of serious compromise.

and pray. He sets us in the company of hot-hearted believers who see us as the Father sees us and who escort us to the banqueting table to partake of His mercies. He comes personally in the activity of the Holy Spirit and ministers His affections to us. He makes it clear that it is His desire to partner with us in the ministries for which He created us. And the whole thing is covered by His commitment of "sure mercy." It's an unbelievable promise, a gift of amazing grace.

## Some Promises Concerning Sure Mercy

Let me list just a few of the promises in Scripture regarding the certainty of God's mercies for us. In Lamentations 3, the prophet Jeremiah gives an amazing summary of God's mercy, extended to those who are in a place of extreme disobedience and compromise:

> **Through the LORD's mercies we are not consumed,**
> **Because His compassions fail not.**
> **They are new every morning;**
> **Great is Your faithfulness.**
> **"The LORD is my portion," says my soul,**
> **"Therefore I hope in Him!"**
> **(Lamentations 3:22-24)**

The mercies of God are new every morning! What a thought! Every day I can come in a fresh way, presuming upon His unfailing compassions (notice the plural – every kind of compassion for every kind of need!), depending on the great faithfulness of His commitment to me. All He asks is that I realize that He alone is my portion, and that I not look to any other source but Him.

In Psalm 106, we have the record of God's merciful dealings with His people who, though they were in a time of great trouble, nevertheless called out to God, presuming upon His kindness. The Psalmist says this:

> **Nevertheless He regarded their affliction,**

**When He heard their cry;**
**And for their sake He remembered His covenant,**
**And relented according to the multitude of His mercies.**
**(Psalms 106:44-45)**

God relented from bringing judgment to His people "when He heard their cry." In other words, He responded when they drew near to Him again after having removed themselves from His presence through rebellion for a season. And when He heard them, His answer was not according to their iniquities, but it was in proportion to "the multitude of His mercies." Our Father's gift to us is the promise that when we call upon Him, no matter what our condition, He will respond to us according to His character of "sure mercy."

Finally, I want to draw your attention again to Isaiah 55, where later in the passage, after the promise of sure mercy is announced, God promises "abundant pardon and mercy" for those who turn from their wicked ways to seek the Lord. Immediately after that declaration, there is a startling passage that underscores God's commitment to outrageous mercy:

**"For My thoughts are not your thoughts,**
**Nor are your ways My ways," says the LORD.**
**"For as the heavens are higher than the earth,**
**So are My ways higher than your ways,**
**And My thoughts than your thoughts."**
**(Isaiah 55:8-9)**

The thing that grabs my attention about this passage, familiar though it may be, is that it is precisely describing His own generosity in giving mercy. God is saying here that His ways of giving mercy are beyond human comprehension, that He is so committed to merciful interaction with weak people that to quantify His mercy you might as well try to measure the distance between heaven and earth! Our Father is a giving Father, and one of the primary things He loves to give is mercy to those who will come to Him in their weakness.

## All We Need

The dilemma I face as I write this chapter is that I'm becoming more and more aware that this chapter alone is an entire book. That's what I love about meditating on the goodness and kindness of God! It just keeps expanding until one begins to despair of ever being able to get to the end of it! That is the kind of despair I want to live in – the wondrous frustration of not being able to find the end of the goodness of God!

Therefore, I must conclude this chapter with the blanket summary of God's giving nature that is found in Peter's second letter:

**Grace and peace be multiplied to you in the knowledge of God and of Jesus our Lord, as His divine power has given to us all things that pertain to life and godliness, through the knowledge of Him who called us by glory and virtue, by which have been given to us exceedingly great and precious promises, that through these you may be partakers of the divine nature, having escaped the corruption that is in the world through lust. (2 Peter 1:2-4)**

Here's the first key phrase: *"His divine power has given to us all things that pertain to life and godliness."* This is one of those little statements in the Bible that are so stunningly significant that we tend to breeze over them in utter non-comprehension. Let me make several comments on the passage in order to break it open for us.

First, the source of this gift is the divine power of God Himself. The Father has limitless resources and has chosen to focus upon us whatever measure of His power is required to establish us in His purposes. There is a little phrase that I have begun to use that is profound and yet utterly simple. It goes like this – the God I need is the God I have. It is that simple, and yet the impact of this proposition is far-reaching and all-encompassing. It is like the statement in Song of Solomon 2:4 that declares the intentions of God and His chosen mode of operation in my life:

**He brought me to the banqueting house,**
**And his banner over me was love.**

I am in His house, and it is a house of romance! His intentions over me are loving, and the banner He has set over my life is eternal affection and delight. Therefore, I have everything that I need to please Him, to walk with Him, to become like Him. By His divine power, all things are at my disposal, that I may grow in a life of godliness and adoration of my Beloved.

You and I are in a most enviable position! Like Esther in the process of being prepared to meet the King, we have been given the perfect overseer, the Person of the Holy Spirit. Under His kind and constant attention, we have been given the double portion of ointments and perfumes, as well as the perfect number of "handmaidens" – fellow believers who will encourage us and prepare us along the way. The circumstances of life have been established before us to wash us and purify our hearts from the pollution of the world system. The tailor-made bridal garments have been provided for us in the gifts of righteousness, joy, and peace in the Holy Spirit. The garments of holiness fit us perfectly, and we will be ready to meet our Beloved on the day of His appearing.

All this romantic language translates into the simple realities of everyday living. God's goal with us is intimate relationship, and so in the ongoing course of everyday life, as we come to Him, He gives us all we need for life and godliness. See, that is the key in the second phrase of Peter's statement. These things come *"through the knowledge of Him who called you by glory and virtue."* I love these statements! He summons us from the place of manifest beauty and manly virtue. Oh, the power of that phrase! Our Father and our beloved Bridegroom are the possessors of ultimate beauty and virtue, that strong, pure manliness that exalts the objects of His affection into His own place of strength and honor. This is the language of Psalm 45 that is so stunning to the heart of the maiden that is summoned to the King's court:

Listen, O daughter,
Consider and incline your ear;
Forget your own people also, and your father's house;
So the King will greatly desire your beauty;
Because He is your Lord, worship Him.
And the daughter of Tyre will come with a gift;
The rich among the people will seek your favor.
(Psalms 45:10-12)

The reality of this passage hits me in a fresh way as I write this today. It is a simple reality yet massive in its implication. Because the King greatly desires the beauty of this maiden, He bids her leave everything else behind and come to join Him in the palace. He knows that the full manifestation of her beauty is not yet visible, but in the summons of the King is the obvious understanding that He will do whatever is necessary to make glorious the one who is the object of His affections. All the power of the Kingdom is at His disposal, and He focuses it on her! This maiden will be the King's crowning glory,[3] and it is in His best self-interest to present her to Himself "glorious, without spot or wrinkle." He makes available to her everything she needs to be pleasing to Him in the maximum way.

The method of this preparation is most significant to us as well. It is "through the knowledge of Him" that we are prepared in this kind of way. I am overwhelmed even in this moment as I consider this truth. The thing that prepares us for maximum intimacy with Jesus is intimacy with Jesus! Through the knowledge of this glorious Man, we are given everything we need to live a life of intimate partnership with the King of all kings, the one who is our Beloved! The message is constant and consistent all through the Scriptures. We come to Him to get the very thing that we need in order to come to Him! How gracious can it be!

There is a most wonderful passage in Hebrews 4 that summarizes this magnificent truth in a clear way. The thing I love about

---

[3] See *1 Corinthians 11:7*

the Word of God is its incredible ability to declare profound truths in a clear and concise manner, and this passage is one of the best in that regard:

**Let us therefore come boldly to the throne of grace, that we may obtain mercy and find grace to help in time of need. (Hebrews 4:16)**

This verse is simply another way of saying that the God I need is the God I have. What I truly need is to be with Him, to live next to Him, to have a place of intimacy with the Father and His Son Jesus that will define and empower my life for all eternity. That's what I truly need. In order to find that life, I need mercy because I am not qualified on my own to come to Him. But the God I need is the God I have, and He makes Himself available as one who sits on a Throne of Grace, so that I may come boldly[4] to receive mercy, to find the empowering presence of His resources to help me become what I was made to be, and to do with Him that which He created me to do.

He invites me to His presence to receive just what I need in order to come into His presence. Oh, I love this! Everything I need for life and godliness is available through the knowledge of Him who summoned me into His own glory and virtuous strength! I am the object of the Father's delight (and so are you!), and He is gladly giving me everything I need, preparing me by the work of the Holy Spirit to be pleasing to His Son on that day, the day of the gladness of His heart.

### The Grand Conclusion

The conclusion of this passage in 2 Peter is astonishing: *"so that you may be partakers in the Divine nature. . . ."* God's goal in this whole process of providing everything we need is that we become fully conformed to His nature as Jesus' counterpart. We

---

[4] as I am, in the confidence of full self-disclosure

shall be changed, completely transformed into the image of His Son, so that we might be the perfect partner, the suitable helper that Jesus has desired from all eternity. What a future is in store for us! What an inheritance is ours by His gracious hand! He has given us everything we need.

Our Father is a giving Father. He knows what we need, and He gives it to us before we even ask. All we have to do is dare to draw near and hear it from Him. My prayer is that as you read this, your heart will be drawn into His presence like never before, that you might come to know Him, and find yourself standing as the recipient of every good and perfect gift that comes down from the Father of lights, the Giving Father.

# EPILOGUE:
## COME TO PAPA

As I bring this book to its conclusion, it is my pleasure to experience the delight of the Father even as I write. The familiar feeling of His quiet Presence, the knowledge of His approval over a stewardship handled well and with a heart for excellence and accuracy is precious to me, and it's the primary reason I do what I do. In the swirl that surrounds my life, as well as the lives of most people in ministry, it is easy to get wrapped up in the busyness of life. There are the demands of ministry, the pressures of a project, and it is easy to miss the moments of reward that make the whole thing worth it. For me, that reward is the pleasure of being still long enough to feel the approval of the Father on the work that we have just done together.

The highest form of pleasure for a child is to work with his father. Because that is true, my greatest joy comes in the aftermath of doing something with the Father that Jesus knew, the One I am coming to know. I used to pray that He would "use me for His purposes," feeling that it was a noble prayer, making myself available for His service. While my heart was in the right place as I prayed that prayer, I have come to believe it is a prayer that does not accurately reflect the heart of God for us. The Father I am coming to know doesn't use people. He loves people,

and desires to draw us into intimate relationship with Himself
for the purpose of sharing His very life with us. Part of that life is
the partnership we have with Him in the work of the ministry.
Like the priests of old, we are called to stand in His Presence, to
minister to Him, and then to bless in His name those who are
called to become the people of God.[1]

This "work of ministry" is not just what people do who are
involved in vocational, career-oriented ministry. It is the day to
day involvement of all God's children, living their lives as full-
time Christians in the midst of a world that so desperately needs
the revelation of the love of the Father. We are all called to live in
an incarnational way, revealing the nature of God just as Jesus
did when He was here two thousand years ago. We are the Body
of Christ, and as such, we have the incredible privilege of
encountering people as Jesus did, asking the Holy Spirit to
invade their hearts with light. This is so that they may see the
glory of the Father revealed in our faces as we serve them in the
name of Jesus. We have been invited to come to Papa so that we
might know Him more and become partners with Him in inviting the rest of the world into His Presence.

Our model for this kind of ministry lifestyle is none other
than Jesus Himself. In John 5:19-20, Jesus is explaining His relationship with the Father in clear and powerful tones. He insists
that the only time He is working is when the Father is working
also, and whatever the Father does, that is what Jesus does. There
is such a powerful revelation in verse 20, where Jesus declares
that, "the Father loves the Son, and shows Him all He does." I
love that phrase because it speaks of a perpetually restful place of
servant-ministry in partnership with the Father. It speaks of an
open heaven of revelation that proceeds directly from the delighted heart of a Father whose Son is all His joy. They work together,
touching people with the healing power of the Kingdom of God,
but in reality, it is play – enjoyable labor that fills the soul of Jesus
with pleasure.

---

[1] See *Deuteronomy 10:8*

I want to live like that. I want to know perpetual rest, constant availability, and joy in ministry that is fueled not by the approval of people or systems, but by the experience of the delight of the Father. I am convinced that in order for this to happen with any kind of power and grace, a life of focused prayer and worship with the grace of fasting is essential. The reality of life in this time of history is that the end of the age is very near. The pressures of life are becoming such that intimate relationship with the Father and His Son, our Bridegroom, is no longer a luxurious option but a desperate necessity. It is no longer realistic to pursue a secular dream focused on prosperity and comfort, with God as a convenient accessory. The Father is beginning to allow, and will continue to allow, the same kinds of pressures that have always driven His Beloved people back into the place of intimacy that He desires. For the follower of Jesus, intimacy with Him and with His Father is not optional. It will be so, one way or another, and my suggestion is that you go to the place of intimacy sooner rather than later, voluntarily rather than under coercion.

## A Lifestyle of Intimacy

How does one cultivate this lifestyle of relationship with the Father? It's a question worthy of some attention, for like any relationship, intimacy with God does not just come by impartation, the laying on of hands, or the release of some gift of the Spirit. There can be a sense of longing that is awakened in a ministry time, or the calling forth of a gift that is given as a tool of ministry to be used in the context of intimacy. But the relationship itself can only be cultivated by the investment of time over a season of life.

Sometimes the simplest of truths can be difficult to grasp, but let me try to share a couple of things. I am constantly addressing two simple realities in my own life. First, I am going to do something with my devotional life from now until Jesus comes. There are 168 hours in every week; every human being has the same amount of time and can decide how to invest in that time. I have determined that the best two hours of my day, at the very least, will be spent in communing with the Lord in some way or another. I am an early morning person, just by the Lord's design in the way I am made, and so my most focused time with God occurs early in the day, usually before anyone else in my household gets up. I awaken early, spend some personal time with Jesus, and then when I'm in Kansas City, I head over to the International House of Prayer and spend the majority of the morning there, studying and meditating on the Word of God, and giving myself to prayer. I am committed to doing that, and in the establishing of that structured schedule, I am able to cultivate intimacy with the Lord. The structure is not equal to the intimacy; it merely provides the context for development, just like in any relationship.

The other reality is this: you can have what you cannot live without. Many in the Body of Christ have an attitude like this: "Well, it's easy for you because you are in the ministry full-time. I have to work for a living." The simple fact is that one makes time for what one cannot live without. If you cannot live without the lifestyle that comes from working 60-80 hours a week, you can have that lifestyle. If you cannot live without lunch, you can have lunch. If you cannot live without *CNN* or *SportsCenter*, you can have those. But if you cannot live without the Presence of the Lord being revealed to you in an ongoing way through the Spirit of wisdom and revelation, then you will find a way to make time to cultivate that reality. It is essential to do so, and the time is now.

Since you have gotten to this part of the book, chances are you are somewhat serious about growing in the knowledge of God as our Father. I urge you to give yourself no rest and give the Father no rest until He makes the light of His Presence burn in your heart to an obvious degree. Ask the Father to send to you an escort, the Holy Spirit who will guide you and enable you to cultivate a life of intimacy with Him in the place of prayer. Begin to pray key passages of the Scripture in a devotional way. By this, I mean that you personalize them by putting your name in the story and by speaking or singing biblical truths out loud over your own heart. Learn how to speak and sing things from the Word of God that would seem egotistical and self-serving if they were not the opinions of God concerning you. He will show you how to go forward, and the reward will be the "kisses of His Word," the touch of the Holy Spirit on your heart confirming to you internally that you are loved of the King.

It is the longing of the human heart to know the Father. The knowledge of Him and His love will surely be enough for us. As we come to Papa, and gaze on His lovely character and His beautiful Son, our hearts will truly be captured. Through the goodness of God revealed in the light of your countenance, the knowledge of the glory of the Lord will indeed cover the earth, as the waters cover the sea.

Grace and peace to you, now and forevermore, 'til Jesus comes and we see Him face to face. Oh, may it be soon!

Amen.

# MORE FROM THE HEART OF GARY WIENS

The following materials are available from Gary Wiens on the Burning Heart Ministries website at *www.bhmkc.com*. In addition, Gary has produced many teaching series and individual teaching tapes that reflect the growing passion for Jesus that lives in Gary's heart. Please visit our website, or call 816-965-9336 for more information.

*Songs of a Burning Heart* (CD included) is an expression of the reality that flows from deep within three artists, whose passion is unified around the person of Jesus Christ, but is diverse in its representation. Born in the place of prayer, the poems and prose, the artwork and the music on the included cd form a sharp arrow that will pierce deep into the hearts of those who encounter this work. The purpose is to bring honor to the name of Jesus through the melding together of artistic media presented in a most beautiful way.

*Bridal Intercession* is a book for such a time as this, approaching the topic of intercessory prayer from the perspective of the Church's place as the Bride of Christ. Rather than seeing prayer as an issue-oriented, anxiety-based exercise that produces fatigue, Gary Wiens presents prayer as joyful and romantic communion between the Lover and the Beloved. The approach is thoroughly biblical, utilizing the stories of God's relationship with His people as the foundation for the contemporary call to intercessory prayer.

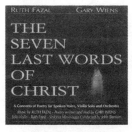

*The Seven Last Words of Christ* is a meditation on the seven last statements of Jesus Christ spoken from the Cross. Viewed from the perspective of John the Apostle, author of the Fourth Gospel and quite possibly Jesus' closest friend while He was on the earth, these poems, with music written and performed by Ruth Fazal, touch the drama, anguish and confusion of the crucifixion event, as well as the tender and restorative beauty of the resurrection of Jesus Christ.

*Before Your Feet* is an alternative treatment of the same poems that make up The Seven Last Words of Christ. The music, composed and performed by Dave Wiens, is edgy and forceful, communicating the power and pathos of the death and new life of Jesus.

# ABOUT GARY WIENS

The love of the Father's heart for the Bride of Christ is the focus of the message God is developing in the life of Gary Wiens. An emerging joy centered in the beauty of the Lord Jesus has given rise to a fresh passion to know Him deeply, and to see His Bride come to her place of identity and destiny in the knowledge of the Bridegroom. Gary's ministry is characterized by the fiery passion of Christ's love for His Bride, the Church.

Since June of 1999, Gary has been associated with Mike Bickle and the International House of Prayer in Kansas City, and is now President of Burning Heart Ministries, giving his full time to ministering to the Lord and sharing the vision of the House of Prayer with the Body of Christ.

# RECOMMENDED RESOURCES
## from Mike Bickle and the International House of Prayer
## Kansas City

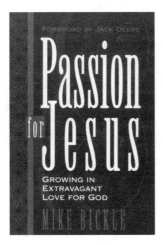

## PASSION FOR JESUS

The revelation of the passion and splendor of God's personality awakens fervent devotion to God and passion for Jesus. This book explores confidence in love birthed in the reality of loving and being loved by Him even in our weakness.

## THE PLEASURES OF LOVING GOD

This book invites you on a most unique treasure hunt, a journey of discovery into intimacy with a Bridegroom God that loves, even likes you and wants your friendship. Dimensions of the forerunner ministry and the House of Prayer are also examined.

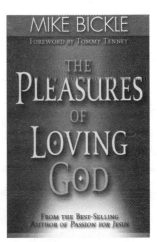